Reading this book is very m
for dinner and a cozy evening of riveting conversation about humble lives lived seeking and finding the loving presence and supernatural working of God.

I've been incredibly privileged, blessed, and taught by having known the Waughs for over fifty years now, as friends, partners in ministry from Costa Mesa to Scandinavia, and as models of Christlikeness. As I read this incredible book of their journey, I was overwhelmed by the powerful lessons I learned from them over those years. Though I've known and sat under some of the greatest teachers in my lifetime—the big names, none have taught me more about Jesus and how to live humbly and faithfully than Fred and Ruth. They look for Jesus every day. They remind me of my friend in heaven, Corrie ten Boom.

This book itself is a lesson in humility and faithfulness—God's and theirs. Their journey is fascinating, marked by a hunger and thirst for God, walking in the light they had, serving in love and with childlike joy and singular passion to know and serve the Lord. Even now in their late nineties they eagerly follow the leading of the Holy Spirit and encourage me to "show up" every day to see what God's going to do.

The Waughs are not "one hit wonders," but incredibly faithful servants and teachers, steady and fruitful, generous and humble. I want to be like Fred and Ruth when I grow up. This book will encourage you in your relationship and walk with Jesus.

Pastor Kenn Gulliksen
Founder of the Vineyard

Forty-three years ago I had the privilege of having Fred as a classmate at Melodyland School of Theology. Soon after that I met Ruth, along with friends and classmates, at Waugh Ranch and felt the love and acceptance that surrounds this precious couple. After their seventy-plus years of marriage, it's hard to say "Fred" without "Ruth" following behind it. This nonagenarian duo has been a force for good to many generations behind them and continue to use their home like a refuge to move the body of Christ forward, wave the banner of the lordship of Jesus, and introduce him as the baptizer in the Holy Spirit. They have an incredible testimony and legacy and have influenced some of the biggest ministries in the last sixty years—always choosing the low road, preferring to stay in the background, and not allowing anyone's fingerprints but Jesus's on it. Fred and Ruth are an example for us all of what it looks like to fight the good fight and finish the race well.

John Ruttkay

A Life of
DIVINE ENCOUNTERS

A Life of

DIVINE ENCOUNTERS

Fred and Ruth Waugh
with John Sachs

Freedom Publications
Santa Maria, California

A Life of Divine Encounters
Fred and Ruth Waugh with John Sachs
First edition © 2020 by Freedom Publications

Freedom Crusade
P.O. Box 2583
Santa Maria, CA 93457

www.freedomcrusade.org

ISBN: 0-9785433-9-4

Printed in the United States

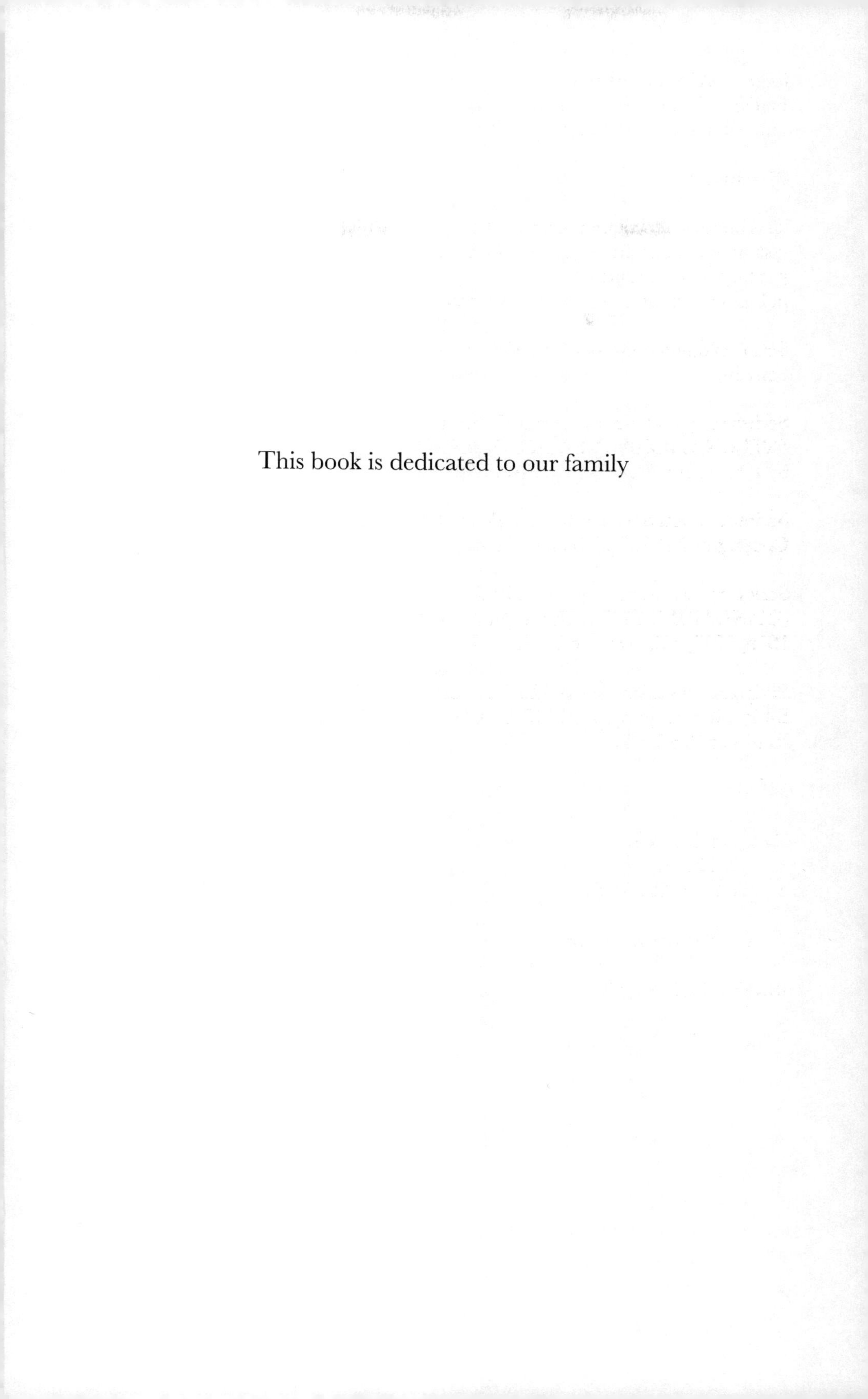

This book is dedicated to our family

Table of Contents

Foreword

IN THE EARLY years of the twentieth century small enclaves of men and women who desired to be filled with the Spirit of God in ways that harkened back to the early church began to pray. And pray they did. Their prayers were passionate, frequently carrying on for many hours and in some instances days. The result of these prayers was neither reserved nor formal nor, some may argue, voluntary. Rather, the work of the Holy Spirit in their lives seemed extraordinary and supernatural. What characterized these fervent Christians was a belief in the reality of the powerful manifestations of God, the imminent return of Christ, and a desire for a Spirit-endued authority to evangelize the lost.

Today, the spread of this movement has become global, reaching the ends of the earth. Some refer to these Spirit-empowered believers as charismatics or Pentecostal or third wave. For the majority of these Christians, their encounter with the Holy Spirit is neither for performing miraculous feats nor for material enrichment. It was a Holy Spirit empowering experience by which the believer could evangelize more boldly.

As the son of an Assemblies of God pastor, my upbringing was immersed in a strong emphasis in the Holy Spirit. A good part of my faith was molded and shaped by a theology that emphasized the refining, igniting, cleansing, consuming power of the Spirit of God.

So when I met Fred and Ruth Waugh in 2007, I discovered kindred souls in this godly, Spirit-filled couple. For over a decade, we have shared countless meals, conversations, and prayers. I have heard about the charismatic renewal—even the Jesus People movement itself—God used them to help birth. I have been regaled with stories by them, prayed over by them, encouraged by them, prophetically exhorted by them, and loved by them. Their passion for revival in the rising generation of young Christians, their stories of the Spirit's manifestations in miraculous ways, and their steadfast belief that the Spirit is at work, all of these are evidence that they firmly believe God's people will soon see a Holy Spirit revival. Now well into their nineties and married for seventy-nine years—indeed they are grandparents of grandparents!—Fred and Ruth Waugh believe in the unshakeable, transcendent zeal of the Holy Spirit to transform hearts and minds for the kingdom of God.

I do not know another couple more profoundly attuned to the Spirit of God and more committed to pleading with God for a renewal in our world that can only come through another Great Awakening. When I think of their kingdom impact over the decades, I realize it is immeasurable—both for its vastness and for its unknowability. They want no credit. They only want revival. God alone sees the treasures they have laid up in heaven over their lifetime. Paul's words to the Romans come to mind as I ponder not only the spiritual labor of Fred and Ruth Waugh but also the lives and hearts impacted by this godly couple: "And if the Spirit of him who raised Jesus from the dead is living in you, he who raised Christ from the dead will also give life to your mortal bodies because of his Spirit who lives in you."

Barry H. Corey
President of Biola University and author of *Make the Most of It: A Guide to Loving Your College Years* and *Love Kindness: Discover the Power of a Forgotten Christian Virtue*

Preface

QUITE A FEW years ago, I received a phone call from Mike McCoy, who is a very close friend of Fred and Ruth Waugh. Even though I had not yet met Mike in person, over the years we'd had a couple phone conversations, and Lonnie Frisbee had fondly mentioned him to me several times. I had also been introduced to the Waughs through Lonnie in the early nineties at one of our missionary meetings that we were conducting.

Now a couple of *decades* later, Mike had recently read Lonnie's testimony in *The Jesus Revolution*, part one of the *Not by Might, Nor by Power* series, and was bringing me up to date concerning Fred and Ruth. They were living in Texas at the time, and Mike had been gathering lots of biographical info concerning them for years. He felt they had an incredible story themselves and that a book should definitely be written about their lives. Since he was not really a writer and enjoyed *The Jesus Revolution*, he asked if I would consider taking on the project.

At the time I was still working on Lonnie's series and didn't know if or when I could ever get to a Fred and Ruth book. But as we discussed things a little more, I asked if he could send over all the materials he had gathered. God had recently been helping me assemble a team over the last several years, and *maybe* as a team we could get the ball rolling even while I continued working on all the Lonnie projects.

After agreeing that the Waughs had an incredible testimony and life story to tell, our team took on the project in 2013. We have spent a great amount of time in their home over the last seven years. I took our film crew to record their story for the second time since 1991, only this time with much more sophisticated equipment and professional lighting.

I handed the initial bulk of responsibility for the project to my son John, who at the time was finishing his master's degree in English and is a very gifted writer and sincere Christian. He has done most of the heavy lifting, conducting interviews with the Waughs and ultimately ghostwriting their story.

As we've reconnected with Fred and Ruth in the ensuing years, they have been a special and appreciated part of our ministry and projects as well, with Fred writing the introduction to part two of the *Not by Might, Nor by Power* series and both sharing their long history with Lonnie at two of our book launches.

Fred and Ruth have been spiritual parents to a multitude of young believers, including Lonnie, and are both ninety-eight years old now, still going strong with wonderful anointings from God. They are an amazing demonstration of God's love and the power of the Holy Spirit!

I pray they will witness the return of their King and Savior in their lifetime, and believe me, as dark as the world is becoming, that could be a huge possibility—and much sooner than many think! Even so, come quickly, Lord Jesus, and thank you for the privilege of being a small part of Fred and Ruth's incredible journey!

Dig deep into this story, my friends! You will be richly rewarded!

Roger Sachs
Founder of Freedom Crusade and co-author of the *Not by Might, Nor by Power* series

Introduction

FRED AND RUTH Waugh were born when the smoke of World War I was just clearing and the flame of the Azusa Street Pentecostal outpouring was spreading like wildfire around the world. The intensity of that flame, and of those who wielded it in his early years, caused Fred to turn away from the faith of his parents. But like a comet hurtling from the sun on an elliptical orbit, God's grace drew him back to the faith and into the power of the Holy Spirit. As a result, both Fred and Ruth have been witnesses to, and influencers of, some of the most significant kingdom movements from the mid-twentieth century until today.

Some years ago, Fred and I realized that we were students in the same Bible class at Southern California College in the late 1970s. Both of us were pursuing the call of God on our lives. We still are. Our paths didn't cross again for thirty-five years, and by that time I had become president of my alma mater, renamed Vanguard University. From the outset of our first meeting it was clear: they were concerned more about our school's Pentecostal legacy than our financial sustainability. If Vanguard will attend to the former, God would provide for the latter. I instantly recognized we were kindred spirits, and since that time we have worked and prayed and rejoiced together to see what is possible when you are faithful to your core mission and values.

Fred is a businessman in the true sense of the word. He has a sharp eye and a keen mind. More important to his success, however, is the pervading spirit of generosity in his dealings. To be sure, the Waughs suffered hardship and reversals, but disappointments both personal and professional have done little to hinder their resolve to support the work of the church, Christian higher education, and para-church ministries.

This passion and resilience opened doors of influence as the power of the Holy Spirit exploded in ministries as different as the Episcopal Church, Melodyland, and Calvary Chapel. God was doing amazing things, while pastors and parishioners alike found counsel and encouragement from Fred and Ruth. In colleges and universities where they discerned the Holy Spirit at work, institutional leaders and students were challenged to go deep and believe big for what is possible by saying yes to Spirit empowerment. At home in weekly prayer gatherings and globally through the ministry of Full Gospel Business Men's Fellowship International, there was one goal: to see the Holy Spirit at work in everyone and everywhere.

It's all here. Fred and Ruth Waugh are an extraordinary couple who have had a front-row seat to an extraordinary period in the history of the church. But they weren't satisfied to stay in their seats. Theirs is a story of faithfulness in action. A story in which I am proud to have taken part.

Dr. Michael J. Beals
President of Vanguard University

One

Damaged Religion

Fred:

IT WAS OUR second day in Jerusalem. I was with a church group, not as a believer, per se, but as a reluctant tourist trying to please my wife. I was the black sheep of the bunch, the only one who wasn't a fanatical, born-again, charismatic Christian.

One of the big stops of the day was the famous Church of the Holy Sepulchre. According to ancient Christian tradition, sometime in the early fourth century, Emperor Constantine's mother, Helen, traveled to Jerusalem and found what she believed to be the "True Cross" of Christ as well as Christ's tomb and Golgotha nearby. A temple dedicated to Jupiter (Zeus) had been built over the sites. Helen wrote to her son, who decreed that the temple be torn down and a church be built in its place. The church I was visiting wasn't the exact same building constructed in the fourth century, because it had been destroyed and rebuilt several times over the centuries. Nonetheless, here I was, in one of Christianity's holiest sites; but I had serious doubts about its authenticity.

Early in our visit, we climbed a set of narrow stone stairs that led to a candlelit chapel. The chapel, made of various stone, both precious and crude, was lavishly decorated. Gold and silver everywhere. The air thick with incense. A large golden chandelier with blue lanterns hung from above. The vaulted ceiling was painted from corner to corner with Christian imagery: a starry sky filled with angels and cherubs, scrolls and arabesque designs, familiar scenes depicted from the Bible. More lanterns of various sizes and colors (purple, red, green) hung in rows that led the eye to the chapel's main feature: the Altar of the Crucifixion.

This was Calvary, supposedly the very spot Jesus had been lifted on his cross. A large crucifix stood suspended above and behind the marble altar. On the left and right of the crucified Christ stood two pious-looking figures clothed in silver. I recognized the one on the left—that was the Virgin Mary. In addition to all this, on either side of the altar, portions of Golgotha (the large rock outcrop known in the Bible as the "place of a skull") were visible behind glass; the rock to the right of the altar was split, believed to have been caused by the earthquake that immediately followed Christ's death.

I stood at a distance from the altar. I always considered myself a Christian, being raised in a church, but my wife, Ruth, was the very sincere committed one. I watched people file in and out of the chapel, and I watched in a state of amazement while many who approached the altar and the icons were crossing themselves multiple times, prostrating, and then kissing the ground beneath the altar: Below the altar was a small opening of exposed rock—the only place one could actually touch Golgotha. This didn't feel right to me. It felt like superstition; it felt like idol worship. I was a far cry from being any kind of devout Christian, but I had enough sense to know that a rock was a rock, not something you kiss, or worse, worship.

This kind of behavior wasn't new to me. I had seen this kind of thing many times before, such as in a Buddhist temple in Hong Kong and in the Hindu temples of India: People bowing down to idols; people kissing relics or lighting candles or incense in front of pictures or statues. Tradition for tradition's sake. Dead-end rituals. The worship of rules. The self-righteousness that came with a legalistic outlook. Religions as ends in themselves that led to nowhere, which were seemingly inescapable in the world. I saw it in my own culture too, had grown up in it. And I wanted nothing to do with it.

The strangers in the chapel thought they were kissing the very rock Jesus, their Lord and Savior, had died on. But why did they think that? Because tradition told them so. End of story. I was already convinced that the Church of the Holy Sepulchre couldn't possibly be the place of Jesus's death, burial, and resurrection, because when I was a child, my mother told me and my siblings the story of Jesus's crucifixion and resurrection countless times. And because of that, I remembered that Jesus was led *out of the city* to the place of his crucifixion; but contrary to this, the Church of the Holy Sepulchre was well within the old city walls of Jerusalem. How could this be Calvary, then? Now, if my suspicion was correct, all of these people, not to mention the thousands that came here every year and the millions before them and what have you, were not kissing Golgotha at all—they were just kissing some ordinary rock!

Traditions like these had, over the course of my life, developed my acute distaste for religion. Being openly deceived. Being manipulated into erroneous beliefs. I felt sorry for these people. I didn't question their sincerity; I was sure they believed, and in some small way I admired them for that—but I did not envy them. I preferred my freedom. I didn't want to be told how to live or what to think. Who was to say the person telling me to believe this or that actually knew the truth? How could there be freedom in giving up the freedom to think for oneself? Or how could something be true when it required faith? All the different religious traditions of the world claimed truth, but none of them could be proven to be *the truth* without a shadow of a doubt. When I looked at all the relics and the Christian pomp before me, the sad-faced Jesus on the cross with his silver crown of thorns, I felt just about nothing. And as I watched all those poor people venerating these so-called holy objects, I felt mostly pity and embarrassment for them.

Yet, I was blind to my own yearning for something more. These people bothered me because deep down I *wanted* truth. Deep down I *wasn't* satisfied with the way things were in my life, with who I was. How did I get this way? What had the power to satisfy me? What was the meaning of my own life? These were questions buried deep within, hidden even from me, until the time was right for them to be asked and answered.

I had been running away from religion for a long time. The irony of me visiting the Altar of the Crucifixion was that all that running had brought me face-to-face with what felt like the source of my own religious exodus, as though from here everything I rejected about my own religion had had its beginning and I had to reckon with it. For me there was no getting away from religion—past, present, or future.

My Pentecostal upbringing really damaged my outlook on religion and church, and for the most part I rebelled against it. I refused to go back through that door, because I felt nothing for what was inside. It was all the legalism, the giant list of dos and don'ts that, if you obeyed, made you a good Christian boy or girl—or so I was told. But that's not how I viewed it. My brothers and I had a saying: If it was fun, it was sin. That's how we saw things.

I now know that my parents meant well. Like all responsible parents, mine wanted to protect their children from making poor choices or from falling into habitual sin. These were Prohibition days, when restriction and legalism were already thick in the air. A growing portion of the American church, influenced by the Pentecostal movement of the early twentieth century, was putting a much heavier emphasis on outward holiness, especially as a means of identifying authentic believers. Unfortunately for many kids, including myself, this led to childhoods clouded by overbearing, oftentimes judgmental parents—at least from our point of view. Put another way: Grace wasn't something I experienced all that often as a child.

We hadn't always been a Pentecostal family, though, nor such a legalistic home. My father, John Waugh, being from Norway, was raised Lutheran. He immigrated to America as a middle-aged man around 1906 in search of the American dream. I don't know much of the history of my father's first years in America. What I do know, however, is that the railroads were hiring a lot of Scandinavians at that time, who had a reputation for being strong, hard workers (many of them were former bridge builders). Soon enough my dad found himself employed by the railroads, which took him further out west into the country, to Montana eventually, to a small cattle town called Roundup.

Fred's parents

My mother, on the other hand, was pretty much unchurched, which is surprising, given her family history. One side of her family came to America on the Mayflower in 1620; they were English Separatists, fleeing the Church of England in search of religious liberty. Fifteen years later my mother's other side of the family landed in Boston on a ship called the Planter.

From New England my mother's ancestors went west to Iowa, probably in search of cheaper, more abundant land. At that time in American history, huge swaths of land were being sold for practically nothing to those willing to brave the wilderness. Her family was quite successful while in Iowa. Both of my great-grandfathers on my mother's side became judges after serving in the Civil War. Later one of them was involved in the founding of the University of Iowa.

My mother was born in Iowa in 1898. (She died in 1999 at 101 years old, getting as close as a person can get to living in three separate centuries, an amazing feat.) From Iowa, my mother and her family then moved to Montana. At sixteen she met my father in Roundup, who was much older than her, well into his forties by then.

Interestingly, the first gift my father gave my mother was a Bible, which became the first Bible she ever owned and read in her life. And it was through this Bible that she became a Christian. I like to picture my mother reading that Bible back then—maybe it was late at night by candlelight while everyone else was asleep, or maybe it was in the mid-afternoon, sitting in the cool shade of a tree.

I was born on June 6, 1922, the fourth of five children: two girls and three boys, in that order. I was raised in the Methodist Church, along with my brothers and sisters, for the first six or seven years of my life. I suppose my father became a Methodist because there were no Lutheran churches around. In Roundup, one was either a Methodist or a Catholic.

Located in central Montana, the Roundup that I knew as a boy was classic small town, rural America. Western Montana is known for its beautiful and dramatic mountain ranges, whereas the eastern and central regions of the state consist mostly of rolling hills, farmlands, and plains, which have their own simple, sprawling beauty. The closest big city was Billings, about fifty miles south. Back then fifty miles seemed a lot further than it does today, so we didn't get out there often. Not much has changed in Roundup since I was a kid, not even the population, which remains about 2,500 people.

There were three primary industries in Roundup when I was growing up: agriculture, cattle farming, and coal mining. (The town got its name from all the cattle roundups it was known for.) Roundup was also a railroad head for shipping cattle out to the Chicago area. The Milwaukee Line, which my dad worked for, passed through town. This was Roundup's connection to the outside world, both east and west. (Today, unfortunately, the railroad tracks that once spanned central Montana are either torn up and gone or abandoned to the winds and animals.)

During political races, for instance, politicians and presidential candidates sometimes passed through town as their campaign train drove them west. These politicians delivered speeches from the back of the train's observation car, like you see in some historical movies today. (An observation car has an open lounging area at the very back of a train that resembles a balcony.) I remember seeing Charles Lindbergh from one of these. He was the world-renowned pilot who flew the Spirit of St. Louis across the Atlantic—the first to do so both alone and without stopping to refuel. Lindbergh's arrival in Roundup was a big deal, really quite the event. In our eyes, it put Roundup on the map.

Because my dad worked for the railroad, my family could travel by train for free. We took advantage of this just about every summer of my early childhood, visiting my grandparents in Southern California. Sometime back in the twenties, my grandparents journeyed to the West Coast in search of, like so many other Americans before and after them, a better, more prosperous life. This eventually landed them in Inglewood, California.

One year, during one of our annual visits, we went to the famous Angelus Temple in Los Angeles. I was six or seven years old, so I don't remember very much, but that visit significantly changed the trajectory of my family. I love history and have personally lived through so much American history in my long life. I am presently ninety-eight years old. Looking way back at that one particular family trip to California, I have learned that Angelus Temple was the first megachurch in America, built in 1923. This Foursquare Church was founded by Aimee Semple McPherson, one of the forerunners of the Pentecostal movement that swept the country in the early part of the twentieth century. In fact, Aimee McPherson also founded the entire Foursquare denomination. Angelus Temple and the Foursquare movement were established in the wake of the Azusa Street Revival (1906–1915), which birthed Pentecostalism as we know it today. Both the revival and McPherson's church made world headlines for their numerous accounts of sensational miracles and for their emphasis on mystically encountering God. Amazingly, as much as 10 percent of the LA population was a member of Angelus Temple at its height.

Our visit to Angelus Temple in 1928 was a vastly different church experience than the one we were used to as Methodists. The Methodist Church was one of the earliest denominations to flourish in the United States, and in some ways resembled traditional European Christianity. Like most of the mainline denominations, Methodists put very little emphasis on directly knowing and experiencing God through the "gifts" of the Holy Spirit, as described in 1 Corinthians 12, for example.

Angelus Temple, on the one hand, looked cutting edge and felt far more supernatural than other churches. The stories and testimonies happening in and around that church sounded a lot like the stories in the Bible, especially the ones found in the New Testament. There was a room inside where the walls displayed all kinds of medical paraphernalia that had been left behind by those who had been healed in the church. It was like a trophy room of past miracles: back braces, crutches, old casts—you name it—all left behind, attesting to the supernatural power of God. This really impressed my parents, especially my mother. As a child, all of this went way over my head.

But most importantly, that day at Angelus Temple my mom was baptized in the Holy Spirit (as described in Acts 2:4, with the evidence of tongues), which forever altered the way my mom lived as a Christian as well as the way we were raised as kids. I don't know if my dad truly entered into the dimension of faith my mom had, but he certainly went along happily.

When we got back to Montana, right away my parents began hosting home meetings on Sunday afternoons after church as a way of exercising their newfound Pentecostal beliefs and as a means of introducing them to others. There was a lot of praying, singing, and sharing.

One Sunday afternoon, the younger of my two older sisters was playing hide-and-go-seek at a friend's house down the street. She was hiding inside a closet and somehow struck her eye on a nail on the door that served as a coat hanger, puncturing and blinding it. My parents were in the middle of one of their meetings, when my sister burst through the front door screaming, blood and eye fluid running down her face, trickling onto her Sunday morning dress that she still had on. Surely my parents' guests were horrified. If this had happened before our trip to Angeles Temple, my parents would have rushed my sister to the hospital right away—but that's not what they did. Instead, they sat her down and prayed for her healing in Jesus's name. And she was healed! The blood stopped; the wound was completely gone. It was like it had never happened. My parents couldn't believe it; their guests couldn't believe it. No one there had seen anything like that before in their lives—a bona fide miracle.

Well, you can imagine that after such an event, my parents and their friends were convinced beyond a shadow of a doubt in the reality of the Spirit's gifts for *today,* which, by the way, everyone has access to through the baptism of the Holy Spirit. Subsequently, my parents left Methodism and started an Assemblies of God church from the makings of their home group—a church that is still active in Roundup today. My mom and dad also left the Masonry, which was a big deal because they were both very well respected and connected in their respective lodges.

Roundup Assemblies of God

We were now a full-blown Pentecostal family. This change, however, came at a cost. Living in a small, highly religious town, divided almost evenly between the Methodists and the Catholics, meant we became the odd ones out. Unfortunately, our new status in the community didn't only affect my parents; in some ways, it was harder on me and my siblings, who had less fortitude to deal with the fallout.

The kids in Roundup were just as divided as the adults, if not more. Each side had its own schools and playgrounds. Kids from Methodist families rarely interacted with kids from Catholic families—unless a snowball fight was going on, which, even then, battle lines were clearly drawn. But as long you were from a Methodist or Catholic family, you had a side. Not so for the Waugh kids. We didn't have a side anymore; we didn't have a group to fall back on; we were the weird ones, the outsiders. My brothers and I suffered the most because we understood the least.

Part of what made us such easy targets for ridicule from other kids was the intensified legalism my parents inherited from Pentecostalism. William J. Seymour, the catalyst behind the Azusa Street Revival, and Aimee Semple McPherson—both of whom were associated with the Methodist Church and influenced by the Holiness movement before becoming Spirit-filled believers—developed that movement even further. Those who believed in the Holiness movement believed that "entire sanctification" was a possibility for the believer in his or her own lifetime and that, moreover, this was every Christian's calling: "You shall be perfect, just as your Father in heaven is perfect."[1] In other words, the goal of every Christian was to grow in holiness to the degree that daily willful sin was no longer a reality for the believer. This meant that the true Christian painstakingly scrutinized everything he or she did, said, and thought.

Pentecostals, on the other hand, uniquely combined the piety of the Holiness movement with the belief in the gifts of the Holy Spirit. We were known as "Holy Rollers" because of our reputation for ecstatic behavior while under the influence of the Spirit.

The intensified legalism was hard for us as kids. All of a sudden we couldn't go to the movies, we couldn't play cards or anything resembling gambling, we couldn't play on Sundays (that was considered "work"), we couldn't go to dances. And since we were the only Assemblies of God church in a town full of Methodists and Catholics, social events in general were pretty much out of the question.

All of this really put a damper on my childhood and just about altogether ruined my view of religion for years to come. But like I said, my parents meant well. They weren't trying to push us away from our faith; they were trying to protect us from the pitfalls of the world, as every good parent is inclined to do. Being a rambunctious kid, I still found ways to have plenty of fun under this new "regime." Sometimes fun came in the form of bending or breaking the rules, like sneaking out to the movies if we could snatch a dime from someone, but most of the time it was wholesome fun my parents approved of.

Much of that fun revolved around our local river. No matter the season, we kids were drawn to the riverbank like thirsty animals. In the summertime we swam and went skinny-dipping; in the spring, when the river was bloated from snowmelt and was icy cold, we dared one another to swim across; during winter we went ice-skating in the day and built big bonfires on the banks at night.

We also had the radio to keep us entertained—that was a godsend for my parents. Before TVs became universal fixtures in American homes, it was the radio families gathered around at night. (Besides, when TVs did roll around, we weren't allowed to have one anyway.) The first radio my parents bought was called an "Airline" from a Sears Roebuck catalog. It was about fourteen inches high with an arched top—a real oldie nowadays. You had to carefully turn a single small dial to tune in to the desired station, about as difficult sometimes as having to pick a lock. The whole family would gather around this radio on most nights to listen to the news or maybe to hear a speech from our president. Kids' programs came a little later, and when they did, we looked forward to them with great eagerness.

In 1930 my father was given the opportunity to transfer jobs and move our family to Port Angeles, Washington. At first my father didn't want to, but at my mother's insistence, he consented to the transfer. My mother was anxious to get us out of Roundup. For one, she was tired of living in a town that discriminated against our beliefs. She also saw no desirable future for us kids. Most of the young people who stayed ended up in service businesses or worse, the coalmines. In those days, there were no laws forbidding minors from working in the dangerous and exhausting conditions the mines promised. My mom didn't want us to end up there, so we packed up our belongings and got out of dodge.

Situated on the straights of Juan de Fuca, just across from Vancouver Island in Victoria, Canada, Port Angeles was as beautiful a place as any to live. I fell in love with it immediately. More importantly, I fell in love with the sea and with anything and everything nautical. If I'm correct, Port Angeles boasts the second largest natural harbor in the world. In fact, I still consider myself a landlocked sailor to this day, forever hearing the call to open ocean.

The Waugh boys (Fred, center)

During the summers the entire American Pacific fleet docked for a couple of weeks in Port Angeles. It was an awe-inspiring sight, especially for us young, impressionable boys. My brothers and I spent most of our summer days exploring that harbor, talking to homesick sailors, eating lunch with them, sometimes coaxing them out of their sailor caps. I once even talked a marine out of his shiny brass marine emblem. I kept that emblem for years. It felt like the whole fleet was my own personal amusement park: no admission fee required! You could just walk onto any old ship—no questions asked—and go from bridge to bilge to engine room. On many mornings, my brothers and I left for the harbor just after breakfast and didn't come home until dinnertime. It was the life.

As far as I could tell, my parents didn't worry one bit about us. (Those were different times; the world seemed far safer.) In fact, I don't really recall being with my brothers all that much either. Once we were out the front door, we were like three caged birds set free, with enough sky to call it all our own. It's cliché—but those were the days.

So for me, the move out of my small hometown of Roundup, Montana, to the beautiful Port Angeles, Washington, at the impressionable young age of eight seemed to set me free in many ways. I felt free from the very religious divisions that overshadowed our everyday lives in such a tightknit little town in remote Montana. In contrast, the beautiful American Northwest bordering a seemingly endless Pacific Ocean had a completely different feeling. My new playground in the incredible harbor of Port Angeles, with its huge ships and fun sailors, more or less erased the troubling memories of some very overwhelming, hypocritical religious constraints and demands for a perfected holiness. This new adventure had become my reality.

Two
Ruth's Paradise

Ruth:

AFTER HAVING three girls in a row and deciding their fourth child would be their last, my father was convinced I would be a boy—so convinced, in fact, he referred to me as "he" in the womb. You can imagine, then, his shock when, on July 10, 1922, out came yet another girl. I was given the name Ruth Elizabeth rather than his namesake, though my father still lightheartedly called me "he" from time to time. I guess he couldn't fully part with never raising a son for himself. Which isn't to say he didn't dearly love me. Like him, I was the baby of the family. It doesn't surprise me now that out of the four of us girls, I turned out to be the most like my dad.

Ruth's father, Lorenz Prader

Lorenz Prader was my father's name. He was born in Davos, Switzerland, just outside of Zurich in 1880, the youngest of eleven children. A year after he was born, the whole family moved to the United States, to a little town in North Dakota called New Rockford. For a family their size, homesteading paved the way for them to begin their new life in America. No one in the family spoke any English, but that wasn't too much of a problem given that New Rockford was, to a great extent, an ethnic settlement. As a German-speaking Swiss family, my dad learned English and German growing up. My grandfather was a wheat farmer, so most of the English my dad picked up early on was from his time spent with farmhands.

Unfortunately, my dad learned plenty of bad language that he brought home with him. Rough work calls for rough speech, I guess.

When my dad got older, he eventually took over the family farming business and was very successful at it. We were the first in town to have our own automobile. We also owned a store in town as well as a farmer's elevator, which is where you would find my dad working most days. If you don't know what a farmer's elevator is, it's kind of like a mill—a big tower with a lot of machinery inside to process and store the harvested wheat and grains.

My auntie-to-be, Matilda Rich, got a job working for my dad on his cook wagon, which was used to prepare and serve food for the farmhands (kind of like a food truck today). It was through my aunt that my mom, Cathryn Marie Williamson, got a job on the cook wagon too and met my father.

Sometime after this my auntie left her job at the cook wagon and moved in with a devout Salvation Army family to work as their maid. Now, Matilda wasn't a Christian, and when her employers found this out, they pleaded with her to believe in Jesus.

"You need to be born again," they said.

"Born again?" she asked, confused.

"Yes. To be born again is to be born from above," they explained, "to be born of God. If you believe in Jesus and accept him into your heart, he will forgive you all your sins and give you everlasting life with him. This is what it means to be born again."

My auntie had never heard Christianity described in this way before. She accepted Christ right then and there—and was born again!

This turned out to be hugely important, because after Matilda's housekeeping job ended and she moved back in with her family, she told them what happened. She sat everyone down one evening (she was the oldest of ten siblings) and shared the gospel the way it had been shared with her. By the end of that night several of her sisters had given their lives to the Lord, including my mom!

My mom and auntie started going to church together, or looking for a church together, rather. Naturally they started off by going to the Salvation Army, but after reading enough of the Bible for themselves, they both concluded there was more to the Christian life than what they were experiencing there. Next they went to a Nazarene church, but that didn't satisfy them either. They were searching for a church that looked more like the one they were reading about in the New Testament, but they didn't know where to find it or if one like that even existed anymore. Finally, when they attended a Full Gospel church, they said, "This is the church the Bible is talking about!" They never looked back.

Ruth's mother, Cathryn Prader, driving

Meanwhile, during the time my mom had been working for my dad, the two of them fell in love. Two years later they were happily married. My two oldest sisters, Margaret Velma and Beatrice Marie, were born soon after, eleven months apart. Lois Ardith came six years later, and I came two years after her.

When I was only one, my dad made the decision to move the family to California. He had heard about all these get-rich-quick stories happening out on the West Coast—which, of course, all started with the Gold Rush before his time. California, in particular, was the new West, the new land of opportunity that so many found irresistible. Although I can't say for sure, I think my dad was hoping to acquire undeveloped land he could farm, since that's what he was good at. In any case, despite being very well off and comfortable where we were, we left North Dakota to make our fortune in the Golden State.

We landed in Inglewood. But by 1923, the opportunities had all dried up. My dad was forced to take a job as a milkman, which was just enough to support our family of six. For the first few weeks, we lived in a garage. After a few paychecks came in, we moved into the house I grew up in. It wasn't too long, however, before all the heavy lifting and carrying crates of milk in glass containers door to door started taking a toll on my dad. He eventually had to quit and get another job working as a postman (or mail carrier, as they called it back then) for the U.S. Postal Service.

Inglewood, California, in the twenties and thirties was a small, quiet, family-focused town. Being just a year old when arriving, I now proudly consider myself a lifelong California girl. I had a loving family, plenty of friends, safe neighborhoods to play in, the beach and the big city nearby, and the California sun smiling over me like an angel in the sky. It was paradise.

When I was five, my parents got very close to adopting a four-year-old boy named Billy, who lived with us for a year. We would've officially adopted him, but then Social Services took him from us, saying our home wasn't big enough for another child to be raised in. The poor thing probably couldn't understand what was happening, why he was being taken away. My mom and dad were heartbroken. That was my dad's last chance at raising a son. We were all torn up about it. Thankfully, Billy was adopted by another family not too long after, but unfortunately, it was a closed adoption and we never saw Billy again.

In 1929 the market crashed, and the Great Depression began. Americans all over were losing their jobs and their homes. It was a terrible time for the country as a whole; but to be honest, I don't remember much that was depressing about those Depression years. By this time, my dad had his job as a postman. This was a huge blessing for the family, because having a government job sheltered us from the devastating storm. We always had food on the table and clothes on our backs, which wasn't the case for thousands of families back then. As a child I never gave it any thought, though I'm sure my mom and dad did, constantly reading about it in the newspapers and hearing about it on the radio. *They* knew just how blessed we were.

My early childhood mostly consisted of climbing trees, flying kites, roller-skating, and bike riding. We kids had to find ways to entertain ourselves, usually outdoors; we used every bit of sunlight we could. I learned how to ride my bike without using the handlebars. There's nothing quite like coasting on your bike, your hands free by your sides, the breeze blowing through your hair, not a care in the world. It's like flying a few feet off the ground. I could ride my bike home from the store with a grocery bag in each hand with ease, which I thought was pretty neat. But my favorite place to ride my bike was to the beach. I spent countless hours by the water, playing and soaking up the sun. I still consider myself a beach bum, even though my age prevents me from going anymore.

Ruth Prader, 1940

Several of my aunts and uncles had made the move to California with us, so I had plenty of cousins to play with growing up. We played games like Kick the Can or Jacks. (I don't think kids play Jacks anymore; they're missing out.) There were also the dunes just outside of Inglewood that we loved to explore, before LAX was built on top of them. In other words, there was never a shortage of things to do and places to be.

And then there was church. I loved the Assemblies of God church we attended. It was small and homey, not more than fifty members. We preferred it that way; it felt like we were one big family. As I got older and thought more about what it meant to be a Christian—and what it meant to be a Pentecostal, more specifically—I figured that if my folks felt it was the right church to be in, then that was good enough for me. Simple as that. It didn't bother me that we were "different"—even different from other Christians. The legalism that Fred hated so much growing up didn't feel like legalism to me. Maybe my parents had a softer approach to it, I don't know, or maybe it was because I was raised that way from the beginning; but not being able to go to school dances, or to the movies, or wear makeup or jewelry, or play cards, or any of those kind of things—none of that bothered me. I was plenty happy. Just because there were a few things I couldn't do that other kids could didn't mean I was cut off from having fun. To me, the world felt like my playground.

Because I was my daddy's tomboy, he taught me things and treated me in ways that he didn't with my three older sisters. He expected more from me. Although that may sound unfair, it was actually to my advantage, because he taught me a lot of practical, self-reliant skills, like how to drive a car. And when, years later, he bought a coffee shop of his own in town, I was the only one of his girls he hired to work there, and I was only twelve. After that, my dad helped me get a job at Newberry's decorating Easter eggs for their window display. He would do these kinds of things for me all the time: recommend me for different opportunities, teach me different skills, all because he believed I was capable of anything, even if those things were usually reserved for boys. I felt like his star.

Prader girls (Ruth, far right)

But not everything was perfect. My mom was sick for most of my childhood. She had severe bladder problems that made it difficult for her to get around and be a mom. Growing up with an ailing mom meant that it was up to us girls to take her place as keepers of the home. In the early years it was mostly Margaret and Beatrice, my two oldest sisters, that carried the load—that is, until Lois and I got to be old enough to contribute in our own ways, like ironing. There were no dryers back then, so clothes had to be dried the old-fashioned way, on a clothesline. It was my and Lois's job to bring in the clothes after they had dried. I remember how fresh and clean they smelled as we folded them. (After I married, when dryers first became a thing, I swore I never would buy one, because of how much I loved the smell of fresh clothes from a clothesline. But eventually I gave in and bought one—what can I say?)

When I was ten, my cousin and I were waiting for my uncle to pick us up from Sunday school on account of my mom's illness. It was a hot day, sometime in early summer. As we were playing gymnastics, just like we always did, I noticed this pretty big family walking out of the church. I'd never seen them before. *I wonder who they are?* I thought. I didn't know it at the time, but it was Fred's family.

Fred's dad had retired from the railroad, I later found out, and had moved the family from Washington to Inglewood, where they had some family living already. That day they had stopped by the church because Fred's dad was going to do some repair work on the church ceiling. It just so happened that they were Pentecostals too, and so they started attending.

Fred was exactly my age, but probably because he was a boy, we didn't become friends. My two eldest sisters, on the other hand, became really close friends with Fred's two sisters. They joined the church choir together. I remember the pair of sisters would go to these Christian "street meetings" sometimes on Saturday nights in Echo Park. The Salvation Army would set up on a street corner somewhere to have their meetings, inviting people to church, singing, and sharing testimonies. That was their way of witnessing.

Fred's family didn't stay long in Inglewood, or in California for that matter. They moved back to Montana once summer was over—because of the Depression. This was probably the first real sign for me that something terribly tragic was happening all over the nation. And yet I didn't think much of it, because Fred and his family's moving away wasn't a big loss for me. Montana might as well have been the moon, in my mind. I was told it was somewhere near North Dakota, but that had very little meaning to me since I couldn't remember anything of North Dakota.

Nevertheless, life went on. My paradise was still a paradise, with or without the Waughs. I was more concerned about riding my bike and building sandcastles at the beach. As long as the sun was shining, absolutely *nothing* darkened my spirits!

Three

Love and War

Fred:

I LIKE TO SAY that I've been in business since I was ten. My father, who had lost all his savings in the stock market crash, was forced to move us back to Roundup with our tails tucked between our legs. The only available job he could take coming out of retirement was one working under the guy who had replaced him after we moved to Washington, which cut my dad's original salary from $200 to $100. Pretty much right away I had to begin providing what I could for myself, which meant I had to get a job.

Although other towns were hit much harder, the Depression had come to Roundup too. Once in a while we'd see hobos and vagrants passing through, begging for food. A lot of townspeople were on government assistance; the kids whose families were on welfare all wore matching sweaters—that's how you could tell who was really struggling. But by and large my family was doing just fine, though obviously we didn't have extra money to throw around.

Fred at fifteen

My first job was a paper route; I was in the sixth grade. I had to deliver all of my papers by seven in the morning so that I could make it to school on time. With the money I made I would buy myself clothes and other necessities. I had that job for two or three years. My next two jobs were working at a service station and a parking garage. When I was fifteen, I spent a summer working in the Roundup mines. I remember being down in that dark, airless shaft, a boy among men, bent over loading coal in a four-foot vein all day. I got a good taste of that world—and I'm glad I did, when I did. First of all, it showed me the real meaning of hard work. Second, it made me realize, as my mother had years before, that I had to get out of Roundup: I didn't want to end up working in the mines for the rest of my life. Luckily, I got my chance sooner than later.

During this time, my older brother, Erik, dropped out of high school, bought a Ford Model A Roadster with his own money, and moved out to Seattle to work for our uncle in the grocery business. About a year later I followed in my brother's footsteps; I was a sophomore in high school when I left.

I was back in my favorite state again, happy to be near the ocean. I lived in Seattle for about a year. For the first time in my life, I was free! I stopped going to church right away, which had lost its appeal long before then. I could also now openly smoke. It's sad to say, but I started smoking when I was only eight or nine, living in Port Angeles the first time. A lot of the older boys were doing it, including my brother Erik, and I wanted to be like them. I was also at an age when I hated to be told what *not* to do. The first time I smoked was behind a church of all places! I still vividly remember my brother teaching me how to roll tobacco leaves with special rolling paper. I was a smoker from then on.

My first job out there was with a landscape company, getting paid a whopping fifty cents an hour tilling flower beds and what have you. That was serious work; not as hard as being in the coal mines, but still the kind of manual labor that grinds away at you. After that, I went into the grocery business with my brother, which was a much better deal.

Then when I turned eighteen, my brother and I decided to move back to Southern California. Now, because my dad was still working for the railroad, we could've ridden the train to California for free. But that wasn't adventurous enough for us: We wanted to hitchhike instead. The one and only person to pick us up was a man who luckily happened to already be on his way to Southern California. "How 'bout a deal?" he said. "If you don't mind doing all the driving, I'll let you tag along. I'll even help you with food along the way." We were dead broke, so this was a godsend.

It was the first of July when we arrived a couple of days later. Eric and I had twenty-five cents to our names. We stayed a short time with our grandmother in Inglewood before moving in with our aunt in Culver City, the next city over. The plan was to make a living out here, so the first thing I needed to do was find a job. The Depression was still in full effect and wouldn't end for another year; jobs were still hard to come by. Some of my cousins worked at the Western Stove factory not far from where we lived, assembling gas heaters and that sort of thing. I remember Erik and I going down to that factory early in the morning to look for work: There were ten to fifteen people waiting at the gate, hoping, like us, that someone wouldn't show up for his shift that day so one of us could take his place. We waited day in and day out, from early July to September, trying to get jobs there. Finally, at the end of September we were hired.

About a week before we were hired, my brother and I went to a street fair in Hawthorne. While we explored, we ran into someone we knew when we were kids. Back when my family and I were living with my grandmother, there was a vacant house across the street that had been built in 1929. Unfortunately, that was the year the stock market crashed, and so the house had been sitting there vacant and untended to ever since. When a young couple bought the neglected house in 1933, presumably for a very reasonable price, the lawn was terribly overgrown and the house itself needed a lot of work to bring it back from its years of neglect. Well, that's where my brother and I came in. The new owners were Tommy and Geneva Quayle. Tommy was a young engineer at Northrop, an aircraft manufacturing company, and he asked us kids if we could help him shape up the place again for a little bit of money. I remember the weeds in the front yard were as tall as I was as a nine-year-old, and I thought, "This is going to take forever."

Almost eight years later, when Erik and I ran into Tommy again at the fair, he was running his own booth for Northrop. During those years, he had worked his way up to chief engineer in the new Northrop aircraft company in Hawthorne; the old one had become Douglas Aircraft after a split in the company took place. "Would you boys be interested in getting a job at Northrop?" he asked.

"Sure, we would," we said. It sounded like a much better deal than working for Western Stove.

Two weeks went by. Erik and I were working for Western Stove now, and I was left wondering if I would ever hear from Tommy. Then one day while I was at work, my aunt received a call about a clerical position that had just opened up in the Northrop engineering department. The job was mine if I wanted it. When she told me the news, I called back right away and accepted the offer.

I don't know why Tommy offered the job to me and not to Erik, but taking that job at Northrop changed the course of my life. Erik, on the other hand, kept working for Western Stove (he later got into construction) and was making ends meet well enough. Soon he bought himself a brand-new car. That made a lot of sense to me, so I set out to do the same; I still very much looked up to him as my older brother. It only took me a few months' work at Northrop to save up enough money to buy my own set of wheels. I bought a brand-new 41 Ford Coupe at a discounted price for $750. The only catch: It had to be picked up in Detroit. How was I supposed to get there in time? I could've taken the train, but that would've taken too long. And hitchhiking that distance was too unpredictable and would likely take too long as well.

The quickest way, I found out, was to take a "gypsy taxi," a one-way, for-hire vehicle that drove non-stop to your destination. For just twenty bucks you could travel clear across the country in one of these. The downside was you were stuck in a stuffy car full of strangers for hours on end; sleeping was awkward and difficult. I spent my time getting to Detroit packed in a car with six strangers like sardines. We drove day and night; it took us less than forty-eight hours to get to Detroit. Boy, was I glad to be out of that car when we arrived.

I picked up my new car and immediately drove to Baltimore to meet a girl I was interested in dating, whom I had met a couple of years before in Roundup. It was now February of 1941. I spent about a week in Baltimore, and to make a long story short, it didn't work out. I drove all the way back to Inglewood, girlfriendless but still hopeful.

A few days later I decided to attend the Assemblies of God church I had gone to as a kid in Inglewood and where my dad had done adze work. I told myself I wanted to go to look at my dad's handiwork in the ceiling, but really I wanted to go for another reason.

I arrived late Sunday morning. The only available seat left was in one of the back pews, next to a young, beautiful girl who looked familiar. I sat down next to her. She had a baby in her lap. I didn't know it at the time, but I was sitting next to Ruth. I hadn't seen her in about eight years, ever since we had left for Montana.

The whole time I thought the baby in her lap was hers (later I found out it was her sister's). During the service the baby's head touched my lap; I think she was casually snuggling up to me. In any case, I left church that day with a girl to think about but with no name to put to the face.

Two or three Sundays later, I went back. After the service I was formally introduced to Ruth. It was a bit strange being introduced to someone I knew vaguely from the past, especially someone who, in my mind, had remained ten years old. The feeling must have been mutual for Ruth, seeing me all grown up. We talked for a while, and the more I talked to her, the more I liked her, on top of how pretty I already thought she was. Ruth was exactly the kind of girl I was looking for as a young bachelor: beautiful, fun-loving, a good, churchgoing Christian girl.

We went on our first date that afternoon. We had lunch at a French restaurant, and then I took Ruth to Echo Park for a rowboat ride on the lake. Things developed pretty rapidly after that. Getting to know her felt very natural, as if we had been friends for a very long time already. Part of that had to do with our sisters having been so close for a time. It was like Ruth and I picked up where our families had left off.

I drove over to Ruth's place almost every night after work. I did this for months. Ruth had graduated from high school the previous spring, and now she was living with her sister and her sister's husband. Her mom had died a couple of years prior after having battled bladder infections much of her adult life, and her dad was living on his own. When I talked to Ruth about her mom, it seemed like her mom's passing was something everyone had been preparing for, as sad as it was. In a way, it helped the family come to terms with her death early on, to begin the grieving process early.

Ruth could've gone to college if she'd wanted. She was awarded a scholarship to attend a Christian college, but she was more interested in starting a family than in pursuing a higher education. And that's just how things were back then: Young women weren't encouraged or expected to go to college. Once you graduated high school, girls were expected to get married. It was the same for young men. Once you graduated high school, you got a job to support a family of your own.

I had accomplished the first part. I was making $135 a month, which was enough—and now I was ready to start my family. I knew I had found the one girl for me and, like Ruth, was living with family when I'd rather be living on my own. So even though we'd been dating only a few months, it felt like the right time to get married, the sooner the better.

Ruth's older sister's wedding was approaching. "Maybe we could do a double wedding," we thought, "that way we could save on time and expenses." However, we didn't want to take anything away from their special day. Instead, we decided to get married in Yuma, Arizona. (At the time, Yuma was a popular destination for quick, inexpensive weddings—the Vegas of its day.)

I asked Ruth's father for her hand. He agreed, and off we went to Yuma. But halfway there we started getting cold feet. "Maybe we are taking things too fast," we discussed. "Maybe we should wait a little longer, think things over." I wasn't having doubts about Ruth, just about how quickly everything had happened now that it was happening. We'd only been dating for three months, maybe four. "Yeah, maybe we should take things slower," Ruth said. I pumped the breaks, turned the car around, and drove us back to Inglewood. We didn't want to get married while having second thoughts. That was no way to start a life together.

We eventually called that first trip our trial run, because several weeks later we realized getting married now was the right decision, and so off we were to Yuma again. This time around we went through with it: We were married on August 17, 1941, in a Methodist chapel. Ruth's family and friends threw us a big reception at the church when we got back to Inglewood.

For the first two or three weeks of our marriage we lived with Ruth's sister and her husband. Ruth's dad was also living under the same roof, and so it didn't take long before we felt we needed to get a place of our own. Our first home we rented for fifteen dollars a month—a price that's hard to believe now. It was just a little one-bedroom place in Inglewood, perfect for newlyweds. The one bedroom was combined with the living room, so it was kind of like a studio apartment in that way. It had one bathroom, a little kitchen and dinette, and a place for a washing machine—known as a "service porch" in those days. The place was a mess when we first moved in, but that gave us the chance to fix it up and leave our mark. Our little love nest, we called it.

Then on December 7, 1941, three months into our marriage, the Battle of Pearl Harbor shook the nation, and the country was suddenly at war. Everyday life changed after that. We had to black out our windows to hide residential areas from potential air raids. One night we thought we had come under attack: All of a sudden, sirens were blaring; the concussions of anti-aircraft artillery were sounding off in the distance. It was a terrifying moment. We didn't know what was going to happen to us. Turned out it was only a drill. But it got our attention: The war could come for us any day.

There were also countrywide mandatory restrictions. Food and gasoline rations were implemented and strictly enforced, for example. They gave us these little ration stickers for just about everything. We were permitted only four gallons of gasoline a week with our gasoline stickers—because of this, I started carpooling to work. All of us were in some way or another expected to make the appropriate and necessary sacrifices for our country and for freedom.

A number of factors kept me from the early drafts. Being newlywed made me exempt for a little while. Ruth was two months pregnant when the first draft was issued, which further prolonged my deferment. And because I worked for Northrop, I was granted an even longer deferment—but being that my job was non-essential in the company, I knew my time would eventually come.

During that deferment period, Fredric Waugh was born eleven months into our marriage. We didn't make him a Jr., which we thought was too old-fashioned for us for some reason. We also spelled Fredric's name dissimilar to mine, Frederick, the traditional spelling. I guess that was our subtle way of being "different." Practically speaking, we thought that by changing the spelling, we would eliminate any confusion between our names; except they sounded—and when shortened were spelled—exactly the same. For the first few years, actually, we called him Butch. When he was older, Frederic wanted to be called Freddy, and then in high school he preferred just Fred. At other times, he wanted to change his name altogether, one being Donovan. I guess that was what we got for trying to be "hip."

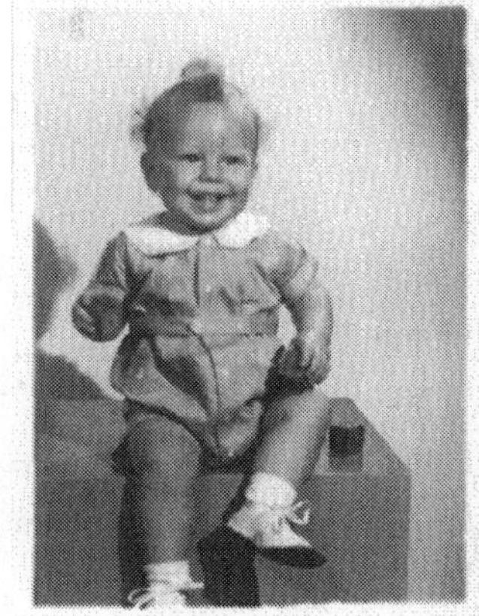

Fredric Waugh, 1 yr. old

Joining the ATS

February 19, 1943—I'll never forget that date, the day my number came up. I was prepared; I had a plan: Instead of being drafted into the U.S. Army, my plan was to enlist myself in the Navy. I was still in love with the sea and had wanted to take up seafaring ever since Port Angeles when I was a boy. If I was going to go to war for my country, I wanted it to be out at sea; and if I survived, I would be a bona fide sailor to show for it.

A coworker told me her brother was an army major in charge of the Los Angeles port of embarkation for the ATS.

"What's the ATS?" I asked.

"Stands for Army Transportation Service," she said, explaining that the ATS had more ships than the Navy, though they were mostly non-combat vessels, such as cargo ships, troop transports, oil tankers, and what have you.

I could serve my country and stay out of harm's way? I thought with great interest. I'll be honest, seeing battle did not excite me one bit. My son was two years old; I had a beautiful wife; I had my whole life ahead of me: The ATS sounded like the perfect deal. "How do I join?"

My brother-in-law's draft number had come up the same time as mine. He was going to go into the Navy with me, but then I told him about the ATS.

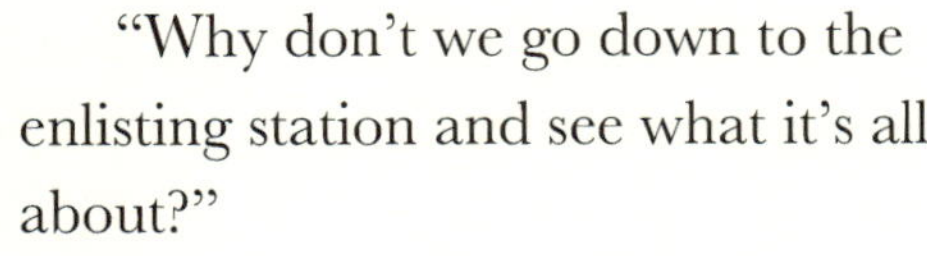

"Why don't we go down to the enlisting station and see what it's all about?"

We drove to the enlisting station early one morning, thinking that if we decided the ATS was for us we could begin the enlisting process. I had told Ruth we'd be back by lunch, most likely. Or so I thought. Before we could catch up, we'd each been given three shots in the arm, our own assignments had been handed to us, and by 6 p.m. we were headed out to breakwater; we didn't even get the chance to go home and say goodbye to our loved ones.

"We're leaving!" I said to Ruth over the phone. "If you want to say goodbye, you need to come down to the station." Ruth was devastated. I felt horrible, like I was abandoning my family. But what was I to do? There was no turning back. Thankfully, Ruth and her sister-in-law made it in time to see us off with a waved goodbye. It all seemed like an exciting dream.

When I took off that first night from San Pedro in the seagoing tug I had been assigned to, it was a stormy February day. My skipper's name was George Emblem, who happened to be Norwegian like myself. Our destination was San Diego, and our assignment was to pick up a barge that would later be equipped to become some kind of utility vessel, like a creamery or a machine shop. Utility vessels like these followed troops around as they island-hopped in the South Pacific.

The ocean was very rough that night, and by some stroke of fate I was the only one left of the crew who didn't end up with bedridden seasickness, other than the captain, of course. And I suddenly found myself in a dream-come-true situation: at the wheel of our ATS seagoing tug. Someone needed to man the wheel, and since I was the only one other than the captain who wasn't hanging over the side or moaning in his cot from crippling seasickness, I got the job, despite having no experience whatsoever.

Maybe it was due to common blood, or maybe because I turned out to be more of a natural-born sailor than the rest, but after that day Captain Emblem took me under his wing, and I became like a son to him.

Our status in the ATS was officially "non-military." Technically speaking, we were civilian employees of the army; we were under the Maritime Commission more than we were under the United States Army. (However, because of the tremendous losses we suffered in the war, Congress retroactively voted to include those serving in the Maritime Service with veteran status, which was how I became a war veteran later on.)

In the beginning of my service I was getting paid thirty dollars a month. (I joked about it back then, saying, "My salary is thirty dollars a day, once a month.") As measly as thirty dollars a month sounds now, it was just about enough to pay the bills back home. Just about. Our mortgage payment was thirty-five a month. (Not long before I had enlisted, Ruth and I moved out of our "love nest" and bought our first house.) In order to make mortgage, Ruth had to sublet some rooms to a couple of young women who went to her church.

My assignments typically lasted a few months at a time. Most were locally based, servicing islands off the coast of California, such as Santa Rosa, San Nicolas, San Pedro, and others. However, sometimes my assignments took me much farther. In fact, my first delivery was to New York City by way of the Panama Canal, a very lengthy, months-consuming journey. Interestingly, the vessel we delivered was used in the D-Day invasion in Europe.

The breaks between my assignments allowed me to go home and visit my family, which was a huge blessing. So many in the war only had pictures of their loved ones to get them through the horrors of war. I can't imagine what it would have been like to spend years apart from your wife and children, thousands of miles away, in the chaos of war, where you didn't know if you'd see another day alive. I thank God I was spared of this.

In just a couple of short years, I earned second mate under Captain Emblem, which allowed me to take classes at the maritime school in San Francisco between assignments and to earn my able-bodied seaman and lifeboat ticket. With this ticket came a pay raise—enough money from my end to pay our monthly mortgage in full.

Looking back, my time in the ATS was definitely a God thing. From the favor I received from Captain Emblem, to my assignments and the protection God granted me, I know God was watching over me. *Why me* is beyond me. I definitely didn't deserve God's grace back then. He kept me out of the fighting; he kept me close to home; my dream of becoming a sailor was fulfilled. And yet my heart was far from him.

Four
Treasures on Earth

Fred:

THE WAR WAS winding down. The Germans had been soundly defeated, and now we were concentrating all of our forces on Japan. With Europe taken care of for the most part, Japan's surrender seemed imminent.

Consequently, I was giving a lot of thought to the kind of work I would be doing after the war. One thing was for certain: I didn't want to go back to Northrop. As much as I appreciated the opportunity, it was too humdrum and oftentimes too political for my own my liking—they made clock-watchers out of you. I wanted to go into business for myself.

With this in mind, I visited a friend and former coworker from Northrop named P. L. Exley at his new insurance office while I was between assignments. Exley, who had also been a building contractor, had left contracting when a friend of his in the insurance business survived a major heart attack and was forced to retire, subsequently selling Exley his business.

"What can I do for you, Fred?" asked Exley.

"I was thinking of going into contracting," I said. "Any advice?"

"Oh, you don't want to do that," he replied. "You ought to give some thought about going into insurance. As you can see, I've taken over this place here—and let me tell you, it's a slick deal!"

It wasn't quite the answer I was looking for, but I told Exley I'd think about it. On my way home, I picked up a copy of the *LA Times*. It was the Sunday edition, which in those days was almost two inches thick. I went straight to the classified ads, thinking I might find something insurance related. Lo and behold, I came across an ad that read, "Insurance agency for sale!" I got the feeling this was more than just coincidence (I would later understand these events to be divine encounters). I sent in my card right away—just to see what the agency would say. About two weeks later I got a call from a special agent who worked for General Insurance of America.

"So you're looking to buy?" he asked.

"Possibly. What can you tell me about the place?"

He told me the original owner and builder of the property died of a heart attack.

I couldn't believe it. Just like Exley's story. What were the chances?

"When can I see the place?" I asked.

The property was in the city of Orange in the next county over. I took Exley with me. After looking around, the agent said I could have the place for $5,500. That was a pretty penny back then—but even so, it was a reasonable price for an established business. I told the agent I would think about it and get back to him.

That was in July. In August, we dropped atomic bombs on Hiroshima and Nagasaki. Japan announced total surrender—suddenly the war was over.

Though I was required to remain in active duty for another year, I realized I would be without a job sooner than I had thought and called up the agent to tell him I'd take the insurance business.

Now, I knew nothing about insurance, so the purchase was tantamount to a leap of faith. I said to myself, "I've figured everything else out on my own thus far; I can figure this out too." For me, the acquisition came with the promise of adventure—the greater the risk, the greater the reward, right? I was excited to see what I was capable of, where it would take me.

One thing was certain: It was going to take me and my family to another city. Moving to Orange wasn't a big deal as far as I was concerned; I was used to moving by now. And Orange was just a few towns over, so it wasn't like we were moving across the country or anything like that. Ruth, on the other hand, I was a little worried about. For starters, she was seven months pregnant with our second child; second, and more to the point, Inglewood had been her home since she was a one-year-old. Essentially, I'd be asking her to leave just about everyone she knew behind, as well as the church she'd been going to her entire life. Sometimes when baby birds refuse to leave their nests when it is time, their mothers push them out: I assumed it would be me having to do the pushing.

Oddly, however, it wasn't Ruth I had to deal with, who was surprisingly optimistic. It was my own grandmother who tried stopping us, concerned for our future away from family and friends. This came to me as a great shock.

"Don't you have a backbone?" she once berated Ruth. "Tell him you won't go!"

"I can't do that!" Ruth pleaded. "He's my husband."

When Ruth told me this, I was irate. At the same time, I really appreciated Ruth sticking up for me.

Looking back, I must admit my grandmother had good reason to be concerned. On top of the pregnancy and the huge financial and professional risk I was taking, there was also a housing shortage going on. Housing infrastructure had been in decline over the course of the war, and as soldiers were returning home and reuniting with their families, there wasn't enough housing to accommodate the influx. It was especially hard for families—even to rent.

In other words, I couldn't have picked a worse time to move the family, but it had to be done. The down payment on the insurance business had been made, so there was no going back. Staying put was not an option. If I was going to be a successful businessman, I had to put it all on the line. And yet, if we couldn't find another place to live, that could prove to be a serious handicap for my business.

Right around the time I officially closed the deal on the insurance business, the agent told me he was moving out of his duplex in Orange.

"The owner is looking to fill in the vacancy as soon as possible," he said.

"You don't say? Do you think you could put in a good word for us?" I asked.

"Sure thing, Fred."

About a week later, I got a call from the owner telling me that the duplex was ours to move into. *Well, that wasn't as hard as I thought it would be.* Just like that, it was goodbye to Inglewood and hello to our new home in a new city with my new job and career—and a new baby too! Linda Rae was born not long after we moved into our duplex. (What made it even more of a miracle was that the duplex owner, like most owners at the time, didn't want renters with children.) It was a crazy, wonderful, whirlwind of a time.

The city of Orange was significantly smaller compared to Inglewood. In 1945 (the year we moved), it had about nine thousand residents, as opposed to Inglewood's thirty thousand. (Today, Orange has significantly grown in population to over four times that size. I actually played a major role in the development of that city, but more on that later.) Our new quaint town was nestled within sprawling orange groves—hence its name. But other than these notable differences, the spirit of Orange was much the same as Inglewood's: slow-paced, family-oriented, robustly religious, and Anglo.

On November 1, I officially opened for business. At just twenty-three years old, I was the sole owner of an insurance business, with very little knowledge and zero experience to go by. Moreover, I had the grand balance of twenty-five dollars in my bank account. That's it! That was my reserve. What was I thinking?

I guess you could say Ruth and I were both naively optimistic back then. We simply believed it would all work out, no matter how much the odds were stacked against us. It never once occurred to me that maybe we were in over our heads. For Ruth, it was her faith in God that gave her peace and confidence, but for me, I had faith in myself. I was growing more confident by the day. Tommy at Northrop had seen something in me, Captain Emblem too, even Exley. All my mentors and father figures twenty years my senior, all very successful in their respective fields, saw my potential. I wanted to be like them; I wanted what they had. I knew all I had to do was work hard enough and smart enough and it would be mine. My father had shown that what made someone a true American wasn't where he was born, but how hard he was willing to work to achieve his dreams. And, boy, was I ready to work my tail off! I had tasted enough of the fruit of success by the sweat of my own brow to want a lot more of it.

Of course, it was going to take a lot more than just hard work, whether I was willing to admit that or not. Fortunately for me, the ATS didn't officially discharge me until the following August, which meant that I had a steady income until then. In the meantime, I worked on my business when I could. I was assigned to a fireboat in the LA harbor: I was working twenty-four hours on, twenty-four hours off. This allowed me to alternate my days between the tug and my business, which was the perfect arrangement for someone in my situation.

And what I considered "luck" back in those days didn't end there. When I took over the business, I inherited the previous owner's secretary, Mrs. Binkley, who was perhaps my most important lifeline that first year as I learned the ropes of the business. I would've been lost without her. In addition to her excellent secretarial skills, she knew the business inside and out and taught me just about everything I needed to know in order to run it smoothly and efficiently. I also happened to share an office with the mayor of the city of Orange, who was also a real estate broker.

By the time I was discharged in August of '46, I had a firm handle on my new career. It wasn't long before I had it running like a well-oiled machine. In fact, by the end of my time there, I tripled its worth in value. Some of that had to do with rate increases after the war and what have you, but I had also turned out to be an exceptional insurance businessman, which got noticed.

I was well on my way in making a name for myself around town. I joined the Lion's Club. Just about all of my friends were wealthy businessmen. I was in the inner circle, part of the Who's Who crowd—and it felt really good. I bought myself a brand-new Cadillac for $3,500. Ruth was a bit embarrassed by it. She thought we were saying we were better than everyone else. But I liked it. I felt I had earned it.

Success is a funny thing. It's a hunger that can't be satisfied: The more you have, the more you want. Yet my hunger wasn't so much about acquiring more money, but rather what the money symbolized. The more money a man made by honest, hard work, the smarter, savvier, one-step-ahead-of-the-game kind of businessman he must be and, therefore, the more respect he deserved. I wanted that respect.

Now, the more I realized this, the more closely I watched my broker friend Vernon. When I sold an insurance policy, I made twenty-five bucks; but when Vernon sold a piece of property, he made up to five hundred—which didn't make sense. Of course, selling insurance and real estate are two different undertakings, but what had my wheels turning in full gear was that Vernon wasn't working any harder on a given sale than I was on one of mine. Eventually the truth hit me square on the nose: I was in the wrong business!

I encouraged Vernon, who was working out of his home, to open a real estate office in downtown Orange, and he in turn encouraged me to get my broker's license. "You'll have to go through the standard two years of sales work in order to get your license," he added, "but that's nothing!"

So I sold my insurance business and went to work with Vernon in real estate.

It was 1951, and the city of Orange was in a commercial boom. Land was being sold and developed like crazy. While I was earning my broker's license under Vernon as a salesman, I discovered something that would unlock windfalls of success and money that I never dreamt were possible: My work at Northrop had indirectly groomed me for real estate. In other words, despite my bottom rung position in the engineering department, being there taught me the basics of drafting and planning—which, to my great delight, could be applied to real estate. For instance, when showing off a piece of land, I could go one step further than anyone else by presenting to potential buyers a detailed draft of how to best utilize that parcel of land. Perhaps just as important as this, no other real estate agent besides me, as far as I knew, had experience of this kind, which led me to become a land planner and not just a salesperson.

PLANS APPROVED — Fred Waugh last night received the Corona Planning Commission's approval for site plans for the shopping center at Main and Ontario. The commission also granted a time extension to Waugh on building the center.

This proved to be dynamite. Very lucrative. Subdividing and planning became the focus of my real estate work. Vernon and I were cornering an untapped market; before long, the company was experiencing the most success it ever had. Not to mention that my eventual promotion from salesman to broker made Vernon and I official partners in the real estate developing business.

But, of course, my insatiable hunger for more didn't end there. My incessant thought was, "Why are we selling the real estate, plans, and ideas to others, when we can develop the land ourselves?" Eventually our business evolved into real estate development. I couldn't believe I hadn't thought of this before. When we started developing the land ourselves, we essentially transitioned from being middlemen to doing-it-all men. In other words, instead of selling undeveloped land to third parties, we subdivided the land ourselves—which I handled and sold as packaged deals, based on my development skills—while Vernon continued with the real estate side of things. This was new territory for a company like ours, as far as our county was concerned, and I was amazed at our success. We were essentially on our way to doubling as a business. Vernon wanted to accomplish in Orange County what Coldwell Banker had in the real estate in LA.

These were good times. We had the bull by the horns. Again, it wasn't so much about the money itself, but rather the aura of respect money ensured to my name. Regardless, I became the very man I had set out to be: self-made and highly successful. I was living the dream—*my dream.*

Five

Prophecy in Tulsa

Ruth:

I THOUGHT I was marrying a man of God when I married Fred. However, he was more involved in his business, not the church. Fred's faith—or what little there was of it—was definitely not number one in his life. Or two. Or even three. It didn't take me long to figure that out after we married. For instance, it came to me as a great shock when I saw Fred smoking for the first time. *Where did this come from?* In the Assemblies of God, you couldn't be a Christian and a smoker. Not possible. I would never have even dated Fred had I known he was a smoker—let alone married him!

This was sort of the tip of the iceberg, in a way. Not that Fred was some terrible human being; but coming from my religious background, I saw his smoking as a sign of his spiritual state. It wasn't a total surprise when Fred stopped going to church a little later, but rather, as with his smoking, a painful, sobering realization. Now, I could have fought him about it or begged him to go, but I didn't do any of that, at least for long. Very gradually and grievously I had to accept that faith in God wasn't something we had in common; I had to let Fred be Fred. I mean, if God doesn't force us into anything, how could I force Fred? Love doesn't work that way, right?

I realized early on that it was up to me to raise our kids in the faith and continued to take them to church. Thankfully, Fred didn't have a problem with that—as long as he was left out of it. I hoped and prayed that by being a faithful churchgoer, Fred would eventually come around . . . but he didn't. He rather enjoyed his alone time on Sunday mornings, actually. He was gone much of the time anyway, whether due to the war early in our marriage, or later because of his career. So I raised the kids, and he provided for us.

That was what was expected of families back then. Fred himself was raised that way. His father never showed him affection, never once said "I love you" or hugged him. Neither did his mother. He was parenting the only way he knew how to parent: work hard, be home for dinner, show up for special occasions.

On the bright side, this gave me plenty of freedom to raise our kids the best way I knew how, the way my parents had raised me. I took them to church every Sunday; I read the Bible to them regularly; I had them say their prayers every night. Some women might crumble under the pressure of being the spiritual leader of the home, and understandably so, but by God's grace I didn't.

Every once in a while, there was a glimmer of hope. Fred started going to church with me and the kids again right after we moved to Orange, for example. But he lost interest pretty quickly. I think he was just trying to make me happy by going. Then in 1949, my sister and her husband convinced Fred to go see Billy Graham in LA at one of his first tent revival meetings. There were thousands of people there. Over the course of three weeks, over three thousand people committed their lives to Christ at these meetings. Unfortunately, on the day we were there, Fred wasn't one of them. We also went to Angelus Temple several times to hear Aimee Semple McPherson preach. I loved every second and clung to every word, teaching, and miracle that we witnessed. Fred, on the other hand, wasn't all on board. He didn't mind going—these were world-famous people he was seeing; they were exciting, and Fred knew that by going he was part of something that would be in the history books—but he didn't buy into it all. He was there for the show, plain and simple. The religious side of it was more incidental than essential.

For Fred, the demands of religion interfered with too much. With his work. With his freedom. If he had taken those sermons seriously, he knew he would have to give up smoking, which was out of the question. That's not to say Fred didn't consider himself a Christian; to him being a Christian was like being American—

something you were born into. After all these attempts to win Fred over, to get him saved, again I could have easily become bitter, resentful, or hopeless (or all of the above!), but I didn't see the use in feeling these ways. They only led to a hard heart, and a hard heart wasn't going to change anything for the better. If I wanted to see real change, I knew I had to pray. I knew I had to serve. That's how Jesus lived, after all. Praying for Fred and serving him was all I really *could* do. Regardless of Fred's relationship with God, he was still the head of the family, and I believed it was my job to honor his role, even if he wasn't completely fulfilling it.

That's why when Fred told me we would be moving to Orange I didn't blink an eye. Even though Fred was far from the godly man I had pictured myself marrying (and thought he was), he was nonetheless the man God gave me. I had to believe that as long as I was faithful to Fred, God would work this all out for my own good—and for Fred's good too! I knew I could trust in God, no matter what. This move was somehow going to be for our good!

In Orange

For a couple of years I attended a Foursquare church in Anaheim. I became really close with the pastor, Guy Martin, and his wife. Fred came with me from time to time. It helped that the Martins were close in age, and it also helped that Fred could relate to Guy, who was more of a natural businessman than he was a preacher—not that his preaching was bad. The Martins became very intimate with my spiritual struggle in bringing Fred to Christ. They battled with me for several years, praying and interceding for Fred. They really had a heart for Fred to come back to God, so much so that even after I moved on to another church, they still checked up on me from time to time. Unfortunately, it was always the same answer I had to give: "He's still the same ol' Fred."

When Guy stepped down from his pastoral position and he and his wife moved away, I started going to a small charismatic church in Orange for a couple of years. After that, some friends of mine started taking my kids to a larger Assemblies of God church in Santa Ana, where they had a vibrant Sunday school program; I eventually began attending too to be with my kids. By this point, Fred hadn't gone to church with me for quite some time. He was busier than ever with his work. Meanwhile, I started teaching Sunday school.

In 1951, after ten years of marriage, we finally moved out from our duplex and into a home that we built ourselves. It was a beautiful, 1,500-square-foot, one-story home in Orange.

The years really started flying by after that. These were the desert years, so to speak. The wandering years. I remained faithful in prayer and in being Fred's loving wife, but I was also beginning to wonder if God was ever going to answer my prayers, if he was even hearing them. All the while Fred was becoming more and more successful in his business endeavors. I was very thankful for how hard he worked to provide for us. And of course, I had the kids, who were a great joy to me. We had so much fun together. I loved being their mom. We camped a lot and went to the beach. We traveled the country in our camper over summer breaks. I was still the same fun-loving Cali girl.

For some wives, my life would have been everything they ever wanted: healthy, loving children, a big, beautiful home in a safe neighborhood, financial security. This is what women like me were supposed to be happy having; this was the American dream. But I wasn't fully satisfied with it. I knew there was more out there, the more abundant life Jesus talked about. I knew it wasn't God's perfect will for our family to be spiritually divided.

As our twentieth anniversary was fast approaching, I started to wonder if I should accept that maybe Fred would never come to Christ. Could I be okay with that? Could I still love God the same, as well as Fred? Would my life be a disappointment? Were all my prayers being wasted?

Then in the summer of 1960, something happened. A church friend of Linda's invited her to go to an Oral Roberts Christian conference in Tulsa, Oklahoma. I was thrilled for her when I heard about it; I would have gone myself if that had been possible. Even though Linda was a teenager by now, I was certain Fred wouldn't let her go. First of all, we were pretty protective of our children and very rarely let them travel without us. Second, it was a church trip, and worse, one affiliated with Oral Roberts, whom Fred disliked very much. (Fred thought Oral was a charlatan; his opinion of him would drastically change later on, however.)

"Don't get your hopes up," I told Linda.

Somehow, by God's grace (and Linda's charm), Fred agreed to let her go. I was shocked. I almost asked if I could go too, but I didn't want to push my luck.

Linda was gone for two weeks, and I couldn't wait to hear the stories she brought back with her about the amazing things she saw God do, about how she had come back changed and more "on fire" for Jesus. Little did I know, her most amazing story would have something to do with Fred. This is what she told me:

"There was a young man who came to the conference whose dad worked for Oral Roberts. This young man, Bob Harrison, was struggling in his faith, doubting his relationship with God, and questioning the reality of the Holy Spirit—particularly the gift of speaking in tongues. It really confused him. This led to a lot of other doubts about his faith, but he wasn't ready to walk away just yet.

"Prior to the conference, he prayed, 'God, I'm gonna go to this meeting, and if I find out all of this Holy Spirit stuff is for real, then I will follow you. But if I find out that it's all a hoax, then I'm going to leave the faith and do my own thing.'

"So he went, not sure what to expect. Then during one of the youth meetings, someone in the audience began speaking in tongues. 'Here we go,' Bob thought. But as he listened, he quickly realized that what he was hearing was a language he himself understood. 'He's speaking French,' he said to himself. Bob had studied French in college and spent two semesters in France learning the language. He was fluent.

"Now he was confused: 'Is this person speaking in tongues or just praying in French?' He got his answer when another person in the crowd translated the prayer in English. 'This must be some kind of setup,' Bob was now beginning to believe. 'I could've given the translation too.'

"He decided that he had to get to the bottom of this and so came up with a quick plan: He'd approach the individual who had spoken in 'tongues' and introduce himself in French; if he responded appropriately, or understood him in any way, Bob would then know that it had all been staged and promptly move on with his life without all this God business. If not . . . well, he'd cross that bridge if he got there.

"Bob went over and introduced himself in French, as planned, but all he got in return was a confused look from his listener. He introduced himself again in French, this time louder and slower, believing the person hadn't heard him over the noise of the crowd. The confused person then said, 'I don't understand a word you're saying.'

'You mean to tell me you don't speak French?' Bob asked.

'I don't know one word of French.'

"Bob collapsed to the floor in a fit of tears, crying, 'Oh, God, forgive me! It *is* real! It *is* real!'

"People hearing the commotion started gathering around, wondering what was going on. Hearing Bob's cries, they soon realized that God had powerfully touched him. Several people around Bob lifted him up and began praying for him.

"Suddenly the meeting was back on! Round two! And this time around, the Spirit of God was even stronger in the room. 'God's here!' people were exclaiming.

"Everyone was praying for each other and encouraging anyone with needs to speak out so that they too could be prayed for. That's when I spoke up: 'I wish you'd pray for my daddy, that he would become a Christian.' Immediately, someone nearby began speaking in tongues over me, and then someone else followed with the interpretation: 'Within one year your daddy is going to become a Christian.' All I could think to say in that moment was, 'Thank you, God! Thank you, God!'"

When Linda finished telling me her story, I didn't quite know what to say, so I said the most obvious thing that came to mind: "Oh, that would be a miracle!" Honestly, at that moment, the prophecy sounded too good to be true. Twenty years without any sign of hope has a way of exhausting the heart. Countless prayers had been lifted up, not only by me, but by others too—but I hadn't seen a single change in Fred. Actually, he seemed further from Christ than ever before. It was as though the more I prayed and hoped for him, the colder he became, like some mean trick. Not that I resented God, but the soil of my heart had become a little rocky, and when it came to Fred, planting a seed of hope was difficult. I deeply understand how Abraham and Sarah felt when God told them he was going to give them a child in their old age. Sarah had been barren all her life—why would this year or the next be any different from the last?

As the weeks went by, I eventually forgot about the prophecy altogether—probably a blessing in disguise. Thinking back, if I would have clung to every word of that prophecy as though I had heard them from the very mouth of God and believed with all my heart that Fred was going to find Jesus in one year's time, I probably would have forced the issue. If there was one thing Fred couldn't stand, it was being pressured into doing something he didn't want or being someone he wasn't. Had I done this, I can see myself pleading with Fred to go to church, thinking that his salvation was just one sermon or altar call away. And, well, where does that line of thinking end? I would have felt that it was up to me to make it happen. But I think God, in his infinite wisdom, had mercy on me by allowing me to forget.

Several months went by, and nothing significant happened during that time to remind me of the prophecy. Then one day a couple from my church asked if Fred and I would be interested in going on a three-month trip around the world with the Full Gospel Business Men's Fellowship (FGBM). Dr. Irvine Harrison, the president of Southern California College at the time (now Vanguard University) as well as the general secretary and director of the FGBM, was in charge of organizing the team.

From the moment I heard about this trip, I was all in. It sounded like a dream. But I knew Fred wouldn't touch it with a ten-foot pole: "Three months with a bunch of fanatical Christians? You gotta be kidding. No way," I could hear him say. Daydreaming about it would be as close as I could get to going, unfortunately.

"I'll mention the trip to Fred," I said to Dr. Harrison, "but you know him. This kind of thing doesn't really interest him. Plus, he's so busy with work."

"Well, you never know," he responded. "God's done crazier things before."

True, I thought. But *something* would have to happen to convince Fred to go. *Something* would have to change.

Six

Going West to Go East

Fred:

NOT LONG AFTER Vernon and I teamed up, we made a pact not to bring our children into the business. I mean, that's a good way to ruin not only friendships, but one's business too. To that end, we drafted a partnership agreement that stated in absolute terms that we would not involve our kids. End of story, right? Well, not quite.

When Vernon's son, John, graduated several years later from the University of Redlands with a degree in agriculture, Vernon came to me and said he wanted to bring John aboard as a salesman.

"He got his degree in agriculture. Why does he want to work in real estate?" I asked.

"He's had a change of heart," replied Vernon. "He wants to work alongside his pops. Learn the business."

"But what about our agreement?"

"I know, I know. But that was years ago, Fred. Besides, what're we gonna do? The boy's made up his mind. He's going into real estate one way or another: Do you want to send him down the street to our competition?"

The whole deal smelled bad, but I was in a fix. What could I say? Certainly I didn't want John to go to our competition, but equally so, I didn't want him to join us. But I couldn't say that, because I sensed the real reason this was being brought to my attention was Vernon couldn't tell his own son no. I'd known Vernon for almost fifteen years. He was my best friend and had never steered me wrong. More importantly, I owed a great deal of my success to him, so I was willing to go against my better judgment on this for Vernon.

"Let's bring him in, then," I reluctantly obliged.

Vernon and I had assembled a respectable number of salesmen as the company grew over the years; we wanted John to start there as a junior salesman, like everyone else. But John was the boss's son and, before long, acted like he had authority over the other salesmen. This didn't sit right with me or others in the office.

About a year passed, and Vernon had built what I assumed was another rental property. Then one morning Vernon and John came into my office, sat down, and said they were parting ways with me and going into business for themselves in their brand-new office building. I was floored. I knew life at the office had become strained, but I didn't see *this* coming.

"Well, if that's what you think, Vernon, then best of luck to the both of you." I felt betrayed and disappointed. I would have trusted Vernon with my life before this, but blood runs thicker than water, as they say. Vernon had made his intentions known, and from my point of view, there was nothing to be done but move forward.

The breaking of a business partnership can be as messy, painful, and disruptive as a divorce. Vernon came up with the idea to split our assets down the middle. He made two piles of properties and told me I could choose whichever pile I wanted and he'd take the other. One pile included the building we currently worked in, which is probably why he assumed I'd choose that one. I knew this, however, and chose the other pile, which included his new property. Well, this didn't work for him, so we decided instead to just work it out between us and continue sharing our properties and other assets.

After the initial shock wore off, I needed to put some distance between me and my work. A few months back Ruth had brought up a church trip around the world. "Ha! That's the last thing I would want to do," I had said. But now, with my head all in a spin, the trip didn't sound so bad, maybe even good for me. I would have a chance to be more objective about the future—and I could do this while seeing the world on a vacation of a lifetime. All I had to do was put up with a bunch of Christians for a while. I could handle that.

Suddenly the positives seemed to outweigh the negatives. This trip could be my reset button, my way of starting over.

"Let's go," I told Ruth.

"Are you serious?" total disbelief in her voice.

"I'm serious."

"Okay!" she agreed. "Thank you, thank you, thank you!"

Now that we were going, the next step was financing the trip, which wasn't cheap. Ruth had recently come into some inheritance money after her dad passed away a few years prior. Five thousand dollars was her inheritance, after everything was settled. When we started discussing how to go about paying for the trip, Ruth said, "I think my dad would be very happy if I spent that five thousand for us to go." Coincidentally (or not), that's exactly how much the trip cost.

I said, "Okay. It's your money, honey. You can do with it what you want."

I still had some reservations about what would be expected of me on this trip, so I went to talk with the man in charge of the tour, Dr. Harrison. I knew Harrison to be a very well-educated and reasonable man, and I shared with him both my reason to go as well as my concerns as an outsider of sorts. He said, "Well, Fred, this would be the same as any other tour around the world that you would take. Yes, we are going to be having meetings with the Full Gospel Business Men as we visit these various cities—but you don't have to be involved in any of that. I mean, you can just go on the trip and enjoy that part of it and forget about the rest."

What a relief! I thought. There were no expectations on me to play the part. I could be me!

"In that case, I'm all in!" I said.

I browsed the trip itinerary, an impressive list of countries and cities. Over a dozen destinations in a three-month span; each one had a FGBM chapter where we would be rendezvousing with other FGBM teams from around the world. The plan was to fly west to go east, so to speak: Japan would be our first destination; and as we continued through East Asia into Southeast Asia and then to South Asia, from there we'd cross over into the Middle East. Israel, where we'd spend a total of two weeks, was the last country on the dock before the trip culminated in Zurich, Switzerland, where the FGBM's annual international conference was being held. However, I had plans to skip Zurich. Instead, Ruth and I would take another month just to ourselves to explore Europe.

Of all the destinations, however, I was perhaps most excited about Singapore, which conjured images of exoticism and adventure. As a former sailor, I was well aware that Singapore boasted one of the world's great seaports. I longed to be back in that world and hearing its harbor sounds: the bellows of ships against the squalls of seagulls, far-off bells, water lapping against docks, the steady roar of a boat engine under your feet. The thought alone of being back there made me feel most alive and filled me with hope.

The Trip

Being anxious to get away, I booked us a quick stay in Hawaii to ease ourselves into the long journey ahead. About a week later, we flew to Tokyo and convened with the eighteen others of our group. The first memory I have of us all together was at our hotel restaurant that first night. We were at a banquet table of twenty. Most of the group were older in age, retired or close to it, whereas Ruth and I were in our late thirties. This was my first reason for concern. Thankfully, though, there were two couples closer to our age.

Aside from this being our first get-together as a group, the dinner was significant for another reason: It was the first taste I got of the religious temperature I had found myself in and would set the tone for the next three months of my life. We were being served our dinners, and as we were getting ready to say the blessing, this character on the other end of the table suddenly spoke up above the noise: "Do I get to pray?" he said. The man, named Merlin, happened to be one of the two other younger husbands on the team. I looked at him like he was crazy.

To my not-so-religious ears, his question came off as pompous. *Mind your own business*, I thought, very annoyed. Religion was fine and all—as long as it remained a private matter. The worst thing a person could do was shove religion in your face. I didn't have a problem if this guy (or anyone else at the table, for that matter) felt inclined to bless the food quietly to himself—he could bless mine too for all I cared—as long as it didn't involve me. But to force everyone to put down their utensils, close their eyes, and listen intently to *his* prayer was taking things too far.

And there was the prayer itself. From my experience, when someone prayed in a public place, it was common courtesy to pray quickly and quietly. There was no need to draw attention to oneself over what seemed to me to be nothing more than a formality, a pre-dinner ritual. But Merlin's prayer was neither quick nor quiet. Just the opposite in fact. It made me terribly uncomfortable, like all eyes were watching us.

What kind of outfit am I with here? I thought to myself in disbelief. I was soon to find out.

The following day we took a sightseeing tour of Tokyo. Most of the day involved visiting historical and religious sites, like temples and palaces. It was very fascinating and at times puzzling. It was my first encounter with just how old religion was in the world, as well as my first encounter with Eastern spirituality. Then there was the night of the first FGBM chapter meeting, which came with its own set of surprises and firsts—none of them good from my point of view. First of all, that I was in attendance at all was not according to plan, since this was the part of the trip Dr. Harrison said was my prerogative to sit out; however, Ruth pressured me into going. "At least go to the first meeting with me," she pleaded. So I went.

We gathered in the banquet hall of the hotel. About a hundred people were there in teams from all over the world. As soon as I walked in, I knew I was in for something "out there" and unpleasant: full-grown men hugging each other. It was such a strange sight! When one of the greeters, a complete stranger to me, leaned in to give me a big ol' bear hug, I pulled back and stuck my hand out for a handshake. *Not me!*

The primary purpose of the meeting, and for all the meetings going forward, was to provide a place for Christian businessmen to share their stories of faith, how they became Christians, and what it meant to be one in the business world. The Full Gospel Business Men's Fellowship International was founded in the early fifties by a prominent Californian dairyman and Pentecostal named Demos Shakarian. His chapters spread all over the United States and eventually all over the world. Today they have chapters in over eighty-five countries. The overall mission of the organization is to empower lay businessmen through solidarity and fellowship to "preach the full gospel to the world"—hence this trip.

As I listened, there was a lot of talk of being "born again" and of being "baptized in the Holy Spirit." Growing up Pentecostal, the language was very familiar to me, but the setting sure wasn't. Everyone thought I was a Christian, because I was with the FGBM; but I couldn't figure out what being a Christian had to do with running a successful business. Business was business, religion was religion. They were unrelated categories.

By the time the meeting came to an end, I hoped that this had been my first and last. Boy, would I be dead wrong about that. Our next destination was Taiwan, and from Taiwan we flew to Hong Kong. In Hong Kong we visited a Buddhist temple that I will never forget. Inside was the largest and fattest golden statue of Buddha I had ever seen. Thick, sweet-smelling incense saturated the air.

Buddhists of all ages presented flower offerings and lighted candles. Some knelt, their palms pressed together in mirrored supplication. Others meditated, still as the statue itself. But the most memorable moment was when this little old wrinkly Chinese lady approached the statue and bowed; she had a couple of small pieces of wood that were like two-halves of a peanut in her hand. She suddenly clapped her hands together and threw the small pieces of wood into the air and let them fall to the ground. I had no idea what she was doing, but I found out later this was a form of prayer: If both halves landed flat-side up, then her prayer would be answered; if one landed flat-side-up and the other down, that was a maybe; and if they both landed down—no way! Kind of like a primitive Magic 8-Ball, but this wasn't a game.

Yet even when I wasn't fully aware of what was going on, as I watched this poor old lady perform her quiet ritual, I felt pain in my heart for her. *This is so sad. How foolish can people be? To entrust themselves to a lifeless idol? To allow the random fall of two small pieces of wood to determine one's future?* I wasn't much of a Christian then, but I had enough sense to know that this was very misguided and dangerous, no matter how sincere the worshipper might be. And were these

Buddhists ever sincere! No doubt about it. But that only made the picture sadder in my mind. I felt so sorry for all of them.

Later on I began asking myself the question, "Why do they do this? What compelled this lady to behave so irrationally? It would be a question that would dog me the entire trip. "Because they were told to do this," some other part of me would answer. "Because of tradition. Someone—a monk, parents, some sacred text—taught all of these people that if they just lit a candle and placed it before a shrine, or if they meditated long enough, if they prayed fervently enough to Buddha, their lives would be less troubled, or at the least their next life would be better."

This was none other than religion as a set of superstitions, tradition for tradition's sake. It was no different in our next two destinations: the Philippines and Indonesia. The traditions may have looked more or less different, but the spirit was the same. It didn't matter if it was Buddhism, Islam, or even Christianity. It was all the rules! The tedious and impossible-to-keep set of rules that always seemed to do more harm than good and that meant, at worst, being sent to hell or being reincarnated into something lower than you were now.

Back in Roundup, I had experienced enough religious legalism to develop my own acute distaste for it, particular to my own Christian tradition. However, I had little idea just how universal my experience was, albeit within different cultures and religions, before this trip. As I encountered more and more religious traditions throughout the world, my distaste only deepened. *Is the whole world blind?* For one, I knew it was logically impossible for all the major religions to be completely true. Ironically, if there *was* anything true about all of them, it was that they were all false for claiming they were right. This caused me no end of frustration.

As much as I would have liked for my growing feud with religious tradition to be my only problem on the trip, unfortunately it wasn't. Concurrent with all this were the insufferable FGBM meetings, which I was helpless to escape. Ruth refused to let me miss a single meeting; no matter how much I protested, she found a way to drag me to each and every one. The meetings were not only spoiling my vacation, they were now causing me marital problems. I began to resent Ruth. *At least the Buddhists and the Muslims aren't constantly trying to convert me!*

I was the black sheep of the bunch, and everyone knew it. I was the non-Christian, or the nominal Christian, or the backslidden Christian—one of those. Whatever the case, I think Ruth felt singled out. I also didn't help my own case by being a big jerk to her more often than not. She never liked that I smoked. Before we left, she had asked me, "Could you please keep your smoking to a minimum, and when you do, could you keep it out of sight?" I said I'd do my best. But if Ruth wasn't going to respect my wishes, I wasn't going to respect hers; and if I was going to have religion shoved down my throat, they'd have to deal with a little bit of my smoke in their lungs. It was also my way of saying, "Look at me. Look what I can do." And I knew I was really embarrassing Ruth, but I didn't care. Sometimes I wouldn't even show the decency in avoiding Ruth's face when I exhaled a plume of smoke from my pipe—my way of rubbing it in. A true gentleman, I was.

Things came to a head when we reached Singapore. On the night of our meeting, no amount of Ruth's pleading was going to coerce me into going, because I was determined to explore the city for myself that night.

"You can't go out there all by yourself!" she cried.

"What do you mean I can't go myself? I'll be perfectly fine."

"But that's not right! I can't go to the meeting alone!"

I couldn't take it anymore; enough was enough. "That's it!" I said angrily. "I'm flying back to California first thing in the morning. You can stay if you like—I don't care."

Ruth began to cry, making me feel equal parts exasperation and shame. I had to get away right that second, but the only reasonable place I could think to go where there was the least chance to be bothered by anyone I knew was the hotel bar. I wasn't much of a drinker—I'd have some beers once in a while with the buddies, never at home—but drowning my sorrows at the bottom of a bottle sounded like just what I needed to get my mind off things.

I left in a huff, Ruth still crying. On my way down to the bar, I thought how ironic it was that in this moment I was running away from those I had, in a sense, run away with. As I crossed the bustling hotel lobby to get to my hideaway, I was accosted by Merlin, the same man whose prayer that first night in Tokyo got under my skin. *Unbelievable! I can't even sneak off to the hotel bar without getting caught. Just my luck.*

"Hey, Fred! What're you doing down here? Why aren't you at the meeting?"

"I could ask you the same thing," I said.

"I came down with some sort of stomach bug," he answered. "I got tired of being all cooped up in my room, so I came down here."

"Sorry to hear that," I said perfunctorily.

"Ah, it's not so bad. Anyway, you haven't said what brings you here. You're not sick too, are you?"

"No, nothing like that. I'm on my way to the bar."

"The bar? What for? Everything all right?"

I wanted to lie and say that everything was just fine, that I just felt like relaxing with a drink for once, nothing more to it than that, but for some reason I felt like Merlin would be able to see through the lie. So against my better judgment, I told Merlin the truth—the whole truth. I told him about the fight I had with Ruth, that I was flying home the next morning because I was tired of the meetings, that I was tired of not fitting in. And then I told him that if I had it my way, I would be out there right now exploring the city. *I'll probably never see this guy again in my life,* I rationalized.

Merlin listened to my monologue. When I finished, he said, "Fred, how about this? We have one more night here after tonight: Why don't we hire a guide tomorrow to show us around town?"

"Are you serious?"

"I'm dead serious."

That was the last thing I expected anyone from my group to say, least of all Merlin; I was under the impression that people like him weren't remotely interested in doing anything that had a whiff of "worldliness" to it. *Maybe I got this guy all wrong,* I thought. *Maybe he's not so bad. What would be the harm in going?* This was probably my only chance to see Singapore, and anyway, I could fly out the day after if I wanted.

"I can't believe I'm saying this," I said, "but why not? Let's do it."

"Wonderful!" Merlin said.

On my way back up to my room, having never made it to the bar, I actually felt a little hopeful. Maybe this trip could be turned around after all.

Ruth, who in her grief couldn't bring herself to go to the meeting that night, was surprised to see me back so soon. But she was even more surprised to find out I wasn't leaving the next morning and that, of all things, I was hitting the town with Merlin tomorrow night. It felt good to make her happy—for once.

As planned, the following night Merlin and I, along with our wives, hired a taxi guide to show us the city. We wanted to see authentic Singaporean nightlife. Unfortunately, when we told our guide this, he understood that as taking us to places where Westerners would feel most comfortable, the "hot spots" he called them. But they were nothing more than joints and bars; there was hardly anything authentically Singaporean about them. We went to three or four joints, each one the same as the last. Eventually we gave up and had our guide drive us home.

On the ride back to the hotel, I wasn't sure if I would be going home the next morning or not. *This trip has been one disappointment after another.* Merlin, however, was still feeling optimistic. He said, "Why don't we try that again in Bangkok? Maybe we'll have better luck there." Instantly the desire to leave for home left.

"Okay. Let's do it," I said.

The next day we flew the relatively short distance to Bangkok. Ruth was so happy I was on her plane and not on one headed for California instead.

When the time came, the four of us skipped the FGBM meeting again and ventured out into bustling Bangkok. I had heard how spectacular Balinese dancers were, and knowing they could be found in Bangkok, I was keen to see a live performance.

I was searching for something; I think Merlin knew it too, which was why he was so willing to tag along. But what I was searching for exactly I couldn't have said. Some kind of experience that would jolt me back to life? Something that could help me forget all of my problems back home, at least for a night? A sense of purpose and meaning? A sense of adventure? Happiness? Answers? The people I was traveling with seemed to be full of joy and purpose; they seemed to be more than content with the answers they had to life's big questions. Unfortunately, what they were offering didn't satisfy me.

Somewhat instinctively, I felt that maybe I could catch a glimpse of what I was searching for in these outings. Not that I would have put it in such existential terms back then; I probably would have said I was just looking to have a little fun. But there's something about being in a totally unfamiliar setting that makes you hungry for life again.

Our night in Bangkok ended much the same way it had in Singapore: Western joints with Asian veneers, tedious entertainment, unbearable crowds. Not only did the night leave me feeling deeply dissatisfied, I didn't have any fun. I had thought that if I could just do things my way on this trip, I would get a lot more out of it. So far my way had left me feeling just as frustrated as before but now hollow.

On a more positive note, we gained new friends and companions as a result of these outings. I had completely misjudged Merlin. He listened and was interested in what I had to say and had come alongside me without judging me—this was very humbling and ingratiating. All the traveling we still had ahead of us didn't seem so foreboding anymore. Now that we had friends, I was actually looking forward to it. Even the thought of going to the meetings wasn't so bad. Thinking back, I find it pretty ironic that the person I liked the least up until Singapore ended up being the person who convinced me to stay the course.

Taj Mahal

Our nightly excursions came to an end after Bangkok, however, but that didn't bother me one bit. On we went, next into South Asia. The colorful, dizzying Hindu temples of India were strange and fascinating, although they further intensified my distaste for ritual and superstition.

Seeing the Himalayas in Pakistan next was breathtaking. Then we crossed over into the Middle East and North Africa. In Egypt, we got our first taste of being in a biblical backdrop. The Pyramids, the Nile River, the Egyptian desert—it was like walking into the Old Testament. Of course, Egypt was just as steeped in tradition and folklore as everywhere else; Islam was ubiquitous. I never did get used to seeing Muslim women wearing burqas or hearing the antiphonal call to prayer from the slender minarets, done five times a day, the first one just before sunrise.

However, when it came to religious tradition, the Holy Land would outdo them all, I would soon find out. Bar none.

Seven

In the Garden

Fred:

OUR ENTRY INTO Israel was kind of a scary one. We had to cross over from the Jordan side. Israel was (once again) in conflict with its Muslim neighbors, Jordan being one of the key agitators. As you may know, this underlying tension culminated in an all-out war six years later, called the Six-Day War, which Israel won handedly, reclaiming significant portions of territory.

We crossed over from the Jordanian side because at that time the Jordanian government didn't permit anyone with an Israeli stamp on their passport into their country. To cross, each of us individually walked a strip of No Man's Land between the borders, where on either side there were these high-tower booths with machine-gun-carrying soldiers in them, watching our every move. Finally, we passed through a metal bomb gate, again one at a time. It was so intimidating!

Being in Israel, I quickly discovered that all the countries we had visited before were but a foretaste of the religious fervor found in the Holy Land. My time in Jerusalem, in particular, was like a super-concentrated version of the last couple of months. Jerusalem is a microcosm of the Middle East. Is there any city in the history of the world that has been more fought over? Three major religions lay claim to the spiritual and historical significance of the City of David: Judaism, Christianity, and Islam—and they were all on full display, especially in the Old City.

To be walking the same streets I had read and heard about as a kid, to be gazing at some of the places Jesus himself gazed at—it was truly surreal. The Bible was coming to life in a three-dimensional, total-sensory way. And yet, when it came to my heart, something was amiss. I lacked the awe and reverence that everyone else in my group seemed to be brimming with. In my case, the more inundated I was with religious superstition and tradition, the more I felt my heart hardening toward religion itself, and by extension, God. I cared about facts; I wasn't interested in anything that remotely sounded like legend.

Unfortunately for me, Jerusalem turned out to be the capital of unsubstantiated religious traditions and claims: Here's the very spot where Muhammad ascended to heaven; here's where the apostles were gathered on the day of Pentecost; here's where Abraham offered his son Isaac to be sacrificed before the angel stayed his hand. No real proof whatsoever, just someone's word to go by. Jerusalem was everything I had come to acutely dislike about the life of the fanatically religious—all in one place.

We hired an Arab guide to show us around. He drove us to various ancient sites, explaining their history and significance. He also talked a lot about the War of Independence in 1948, the year Israel won its nationhood back from the Arabs. He pointed out bombed-out weapons carriers and military vehicles and tanks.

"People don't live in these houses anymore," he said as we drove past an empty neighborhood. "We want to leave them that way so when the people come back, they'll have their homes again." So sad what war does to people.

One of the stops I remember the most was connected to a war story that sounded a little too fantastical for me to believe outright. According to our guide, during the war, a Jewish soldier, with only a pitchfork in hand, took on and defeated an enemy machine gun nest all by himself—and survived. *That's impossible,* I thought. *How could anyone believe that?* It had the air of a story one would find in the Old Testament but with a modern backdrop. The problem was this wasn't some story lost to ancient history. The war had taken place thirteen years prior, so where was the historical evidence to support such a courageous feat? Were there newspaper clippings I could see? Living eyewitnesses? How was I supposed to believe this—because a tour guide told me so? And say the story *was* true, exactly as the man had told it—what did that mean? Was it an act of God? It sure sounded like that's what our guide wanted us to believe, despite the fact he was a Muslim. I knew there was no way for me to get to the bottom of these answers. That's what was so frustrating. My overly rationalistic brain didn't know what to do with a place where history and myth were so seemingly inextricably bound.

One day we followed a group of pilgrims around as they were celebrating "the Way of the Cross." They must have been Catholic or Orthodox in faith. In any case, "the Way of the Cross" is a ritualistic reenactment of the fourteen stations of the Christ's Passion, each one commemorating a significant moment in the narrative, from his sentencing before Pilate to his crucifixion. These pilgrims actually carried a life-size wooden cross with them. The whole time I was thinking, *How do they know this is where Jesus fell for the first time? How do they know this is where Simon the Cyrene helped Jesus carry his cross?* On and on and on. Of course, there was only one answer to this: tradition. But how unsatisfying, unreliable.

When we made it to the Church of the Holy Sepulchre, things got even more confusing and frustrating. The church, which concluded the journey with stations eleven through fourteen, allegedly housed both Jesus's place of crucifixion and burial. But I knew better. I was well aware beforehand that Jesus had been taken *outside* the walls of Jerusalem to be crucified and that, in clear-as-day contradiction to this, the Church of the Holy Sepulchre was well within those walls. *This is blind tradition at its worst,* I thought. *This is exploitation. All of these people are worshipping icons and rocks, and they're being told if they touch this sacred object or kiss that sacred object, they will be blessed. This is classic idolatry. How is this any different from praying to a statue of Buddha or worshipping one of the Hindu idols?*

Strangely, Ruth and the rest of the group appeared to be going right along with the ride—as if it were all true! *How could they be so naïve?* Granted, they weren't going so far as to prostrate themselves or venerate the icons, but I could see they were impressed, to say the least. *Was I the only one in this ancient city with some sense?*

After we visited Calvary, we made our way to the other end of the church, to the Rotunda, where Christ's tomb was allegedly located. Calvary and the tomb were less than two hundred feet apart. Fighting the crowds, we stepped into a large circular space filled with natural light that streamed in from the high-domed ceiling several stories above. Stone pillars encircled the room, supporting the only structure that dated back to Constantine's original church. In the center of the Rotunda, standing like an island, stood the Edicule—the shrine built over top of Christ's tomb. It looked like a very old, small stone chapel with a balcony-like roof and a cupola on top. People were circling the Edicule like a human whirlpool. At the entrance to the tomb, there was a small ornately adorned door, decorated in the same fashion as the Altar of the Crucifixion. Inside the Edicule there were two rooms: the front room (the Chapel of the Angel), which was open to the public and the bigger of the two rooms; and the second room, Christ's tomb itself, also known as the Holy Sepulchre, which was sealed off to the public.

For millions of Christians around the world this was the holiest place on earth, where Jesus literally rose from the dead. Relics abounded. In the Chapel of the Angel, there was the Angel's Rock—a fragment of the large stone that originally sealed Christ's tomb, which, as the story goes, "the angel of the Lord" rolled back. Just as they did at Golgotha, worshippers bowed before this stone, kissed it, and did the sign of the cross over themselves several times. Once again I was filled with disdain as I watched people demean themselves in the name of blind tradition. *How much more of this will I have to endure? How can these people be certain this rock was part of the same rock that sealed Christ's tomb?*

Around every corner, the church seemed to be filled with legends: Here's where Adam was buried; here's where Jesus's dead body was prepared for burial; here's where Helen, Constantine's mother, found the three crosses. Some of the traditions were blatantly wrong. For example, in the Catholicon, the large Greek Orthodox sanctuary next to the Rotunda, there was a stone there put in place in medieval times that marked what was believed to be the geographical epicenter of the known world. But maps today obviously disprove this. But even if this stone was no longer believed to be the center of the physical world, but rather of the spiritual world, how could *that* even be believed if this church wasn't the actual location of Jesus's death and resurrection? And if some of the traditions being touted were fraudulent, how could any of them be trusted? For me, the only thing the Church of the Holy Sepulchre could be called the center of was the center of religious hoaxes.

By the time we left, I didn't want to see another so-called holy site. I'd seen enough that day alone for a lifetime. But I knew much more was on the way. On another day, we visited the Church of All Nations, which the Roman Catholics built and presided over, although a number of other churches also used it. The church was located in the Mount of Olives adjacent to the garden of Gethsemane, where Jesus spent his last night praying and where he was arrested. It was a beautiful stone church with four Corinthian-styled columns dominating the church's façade, each one topped with a statue of one of the Four Evangelists. Above them, a beautiful mosaic of Jesus, as mediator between God and man, spanned the top half of the church's façade. There were many more columns inside and a vaulted, bubble-domed, starry blue ceiling. Most importantly, though, at the back of the church, in front of the open altar, was a large piece of bedrock enshrined by a low fence shaped after the crown of thorns Jesus had worn. According to tradition, this was where Jesus knelt to pray, his sweat like drops of blood.

When we walked in, there was another FGBM group of about fifty people already inside. Then someone from the other group had the idea of leading an impromptu worship service for the combined groups. Since I wasn't much for singing hymns, I used my time to people-watch. I noticed a man from the other group worshipping in a way that intrigued me. (Later I found out he was a Presbyterian theologian from Pennsylvania.) He wasn't being showy or displaying any kind of emotionalism; his worship looked sincere, heartfelt, quiet. He was totally immersed in the moment and in the setting. In contrast to those at the Holy Sepulchre and elsewhere, this man looked free. It was the first time I could say that I was actually watching someone worship God in spirit and in truth (though I wouldn't have put it that way back then). On his face he wore the perfect expression of peace and joy. The more I watched him, the more I was mesmerized. If he had begun to ascend, I wouldn't have been surprised.

Interestingly, I found myself envious of this man; I wanted to experience what he was experiencing. He was "somewhere else." (Now, if I had been as familiar with the Bible as I am now, I would've likened it to Paul's vision of the "third heaven" that he describes in his second letter to the Corinthians.) *What this man is experiencing—is that what I've been searching for?* I was almost certain I had never felt the way this man looked to be feeling. It was the first time in a long time—maybe the first time ever, certainly that I could recall—that I truly desired to experience God. Most importantly, what he was experiencing seemed to have little to nothing to do with religion, and to my surprise I was drawn to that.

Later that day we visited the Garden Tomb—another purported site of Jesus's burial and resurrection. *How many of these places are there?* A narrow path led into the garden. It was beautiful, lush, and manicured inside, just how I imagined scenes from the Bible looking. I walked along a small ridge, and off to one side of the garden, down below, was Christ's tomb. It certainly had the look of the tomb described in the Gospels: It was built into the face of a rock wall that strikingly resembled a skull; a small rectangular opening led inside. There wasn't much to see once inside, however, just a close-cramped, mostly empty room carved out of the rock with a shallow impression where the body would've been laid. To be honest, I was more impressed with the garden right outside.

The Garden Tomb

The Garden Tomb was discovered in the mid-nineteenth century as an alternative location of Christ's burial. As the garden garnered attention, many more endorsed it, believing that the Church of the Holy Sepulchre couldn't possibly be the location of Christ's death and resurrection, since it was within the walls of Old Jerusalem. Unlike the overcrowded, stuffy, and gloomy Holy Sepulchre, the Garden Tomb was peaceful and natural. Gravel paths guided you through flower beds and ferns, over stone bridges, and under clusters of trees. If there ever was a place to pray, this was it.

My mind was still reeling from my time at the Church of All Nations, still thinking about that man who had been "caught up," still feeling the ripples of my envy. What was happening to me? Just yesterday I was more convinced than ever that religion wasn't for me, that there was no way of knowing for certain the kind of truths religions claimed about reality. But seeing that man, it was as if I had taken a sudden, unexpected turn from the highway down a narrow, winding road—and where this road led, I had no idea. Was this beautiful garden the end of that "road"?

My head was full of warring thoughts. Something had changed in me ever so slightly; a crack had formed in the foundation of the wall I had built to keep myself from God. What was it about this garden that seemed to be speaking to me? There was a still, small voice all around me, in the wind and in the rocks and in the trees and flowers.

Just then, a different kind of voice spoke up, one that I was very familiar with: "How do you *actually* know this is the real burial grounds of Jesus?"

"I don't know," I thought back.

"Exactly. Don't be fooled by the tranquility and beauty of this place. It's just a veneer; underneath is just more empty tradition. More religion. More superstition. If it's not fact, it's not worth trusting—remember?"

This was my inner voice speaking, my own rational way of thinking, trying to reassert dominance. Had my emotions gotten the better of me? Had my time in Jerusalem finally hoodwinked me? Surely I shouldn't have to justify what I already knew to be true of myself: why I lived the way I did, how I rationalized everything, why I didn't go to church, why I didn't pray or read the Bible. But here now I was doing just that. Did I really want to go back to all that legalism? Did I really want to forfeit my freedom? I couldn't become a Christian—a real Christian. I looked down on Christians. I pitied them. They were slaves to their rituals and traditions; religion was their crutch. As for me, I had done quite well for myself without religion. I was a self-made man. I didn't need God to get my act straight. I didn't need him in order to be a decent human being or to be successful. I had accomplished all that on my own.

And yet, for once, there was a part of me that didn't want to listen to *my* voice anymore. *Hang up the phone!* Part of me wanted to see where this other train of thought, this other "voice," would take me.

Suddenly that silent voice I sensed all around spoke: "You're just as bad as they are."

"As who?" I asked.

"You're judging all of these people for blindly following tradition," the voice continued, "but you've been blindly following your own traditions, you've been worshipping your own set of rules. You believe that if you can't see it, then it's not real, or if it can't be proven, then it's false. But you're missing the whole point: It's not about knowing facts—it's about finding me."

"And who are *you*?"

"I am the Truth you've been looking for—but you keep rejecting me because you see me as no more than a bunch of rules and rituals. That's not what following me is all about. Following me is just as natural and beautiful as this garden, as these flowers and these trees that have sprouted from the ground, as the air you breathe. But you were right about one thing: Being a Christian isn't about following tradition for tradition's sake, whether that be your own made-up tradition or a tradition thousands of years old."

"What is it about, then?"

"It's about accepting what I've done for you. It's about believing that I died for you. That I love you."

"But what about all the stuff in my life that you don't like? My smoking. My drinking. Don't these things keep me from getting into heaven?"

"I am the true heaven. Am I not with you *now*, speaking right into your heart? I'm not telling you to do anything other than to believe in me and to believe what I did for you on the cross, to accept eternal life by having a relationship with me. It is only your unbelief that keeps you from knowing me. If you humble yourself, I can save you. Then the joy and the peace and the love you saw in that man you so envied will be yours too—for I am these things. But you must *let me in*; I will take care of the rest. I can wash you clean; I can make your heart into a garden springing up into eternity, where death and disease have no place."

Well, if that's all that's required of me! I thought, totally amazed.

Not knowing what else to do, I decided to pray a simple prayer: "God, if what I'm feeling in my heart is right and real, then I want you to make it real in my life—real like that man worshipping you in the church knew it was real."

Suddenly it was as if a flame kindled deep within the recesses of my heart, and from there, the light and warmth of that flame slowly spread outward, filling up my whole body. Before I knew it, my eyes were opened! Being a Christian wasn't about believing in a God who loved you *only if* you obeyed all of his commandments. Rather, it was about being in a personal relationship with God himself—who already loved me. He loved me to the point of dying on a cross! Smoking, drinking, gambling—these things didn't damn you. What condemns a person is rejecting God's gifts, his Son and his Spirit, that's what leads to death. It is like starving tree roots rejecting rain. All God was asking of me, all he had ever been asking of me, was to get to know his Son. To walk with him in his garden.

Fred's "birthplace"

Eight

The Forgotten Third Person

Ruth:

TWENTY YEARS of not knowing if Fred would ever find God was a long time to wait. No longer young, it was hard for me to even imagine a different kind of Fred other than the one I had always known. It was very discouraging at times, but that never stopped me from praying. As I've said before, prayer was all I had: As long as I had that, there was always hope, a ray of sunlight cutting through dark gray clouds, keeping my gaze upwards.

By the time we reached Singapore, my life was feeling dark and lonely; my closeness with Fred was at an all-time low. But when I least expected it, several unexpected "rays of light" broke through, the first being Fred's unlikely friendship with Merlin, which kept him from leaving. Then, after Thailand, another ray beamed down: I no longer had to drag Fred to the meetings, which was such a relief! He was going willingly, even happily! I was so thrilled!

As we were strolling through the Garden Tomb, I felt in my soul that God was working on Fred. How did I know? I saw it in his thoughtful face and in his slow, meandering walk. I wanted to say something, but out of respect, I didn't; I just let him be. Plus, I wasn't *completely* certain I was right, nor did I know just how much God had broken through.

I got pretty sick the next day, enough that I had to stay in and miss the meeting that night. I really hated missing meetings, but at least I would have Fred to keep me company—or so I thought. To my surprise he asked, "Do you mind if I still go?"

"You want to go without me?" I responded, unsure if I had heard him right.

"Is that okay? I don't have to go if you don't want me to."

I couldn't believe my ears. I wanted to leap into his arms and kiss him. But knowing Fred, it wasn't smart to make a big deal out of things, so I said, "Of course you can go. I'll be fine here."

Later that evening, with Fred gone, I lay on my bed thinking, *Oh, God! You did it! You did it! You did it! Thank you, thank you, thank you!* So many years of hoping and praying and waiting for something, for *anything*, to happen, for God to grab hold of my husband and set him free! All those countless prayers were finally being answered: *Fred went to a meeting all on his own! It's a miracle! Is this really happening? Should I pinch myself?*

I was so relieved, so overjoyed, so thankful; I no longer cared that I was sick and missing the meeting. Actually, I was glad I got sick, because if I hadn't, Fred wouldn't have asked to go alone.

When Fred got back, I asked him how it went.

"It was good," was all he said.

I wanted so badly to ask more, but I left it at that. I didn't want to push my luck (even though I knew luck had nothing to do with it). Fred would open up to me when he was ready, and anyway, after twenty years I could be patient a little longer.

The following Sunday was Pentecost Sunday, and we went to a Pentecostal church to celebrate the feast. The pastor spoke on the Holy Spirit and the purpose of speaking in tongues. Then it came time to take Communion. When the plate of crackers was being passed around (crackers and grape juice are the traditions of the Pentecostal church when taking Communion), I wondered if Fred would take one. He didn't. The juice followed immediately after, bouncing in their tiny clear cups. Unsurprisingly, Fred didn't take one of those either. *I bet he's being too shy or respectful to take Communion*, I thought. So I broke my cracker in two and offered half to Fred. I saw in his eyes the realization that I *knew*, that there was no point in hiding his faith anymore. With a smile, he took the cracker piece and ate. We took Communion together for the first time! It was so beautiful! I love that Communion turned out to be Fred's way of opening up to me. The moment didn't need words. The Body and the Blood were enough.

Later on, Fred explained why he didn't take Communion initially: "I wanted to take Communion so badly that I could almost taste the cracker and the juice as they went by; but I knew everyone in our group was hoping and praying for this to happen, most of all you, Ruth, and I didn't want to draw too much attention to myself. I was still processing what had happened. By taking Communion, I'd be giving myself away, essentially saying, 'Hey, everyone! I believe now. I'm a Christian!' and that would've made everything suddenly about me. Others might expect too much from me once they found out or scrutinize my actions more closely. I also remembered the scripture that said not to take Communion in an unworthy manner, that I needed to examine my heart closely, otherwise I might eat and drink judgment. I didn't know what that meant exactly, so I thought I should hold off for now, just to be safe. When I saw you offer me some of your cracker, I was so relieved! *She already knows!* A spirit of freedom came over me—like I could finally be myself!"

I told Fred no one was going to tell him how to be or how to act, least of all me: "We all love you. The angels in heaven are dancing because of you. We just want the opportunity to dance with them before the party's over."

From this point forward Fred and I started doing something we had never done before as a couple, something I had always dreamed of doing with him: We read the Bible together. And what a glorious experience that was! It's probably hard for some people to understand just how relieved and happy I was to be reading the Bible with my husband, as simple as that sounds; but as someone who had been doing her daily devotions year after year after year alone, I knew something was glaringly missing all that time—or more like *someone*.

Now my dream of reading the Bible with my husband had come true! Now I had someone to discuss God with. Now I had someone to dive into the heart of God with. We were finally united in Christ—together! It says in the Bible that where two or more are gathered in Jesus's name, there he is. Well, there were two of us now, all the time. There was a lot more "room" for Christ in our house, in our lives, because we welcomed him together. God could now breathe his love and grace through us as one unit, as one "flesh," just as he intended our marriage to be; and at last Fred assumed the mantle of spiritual leader of the family, the mantle I had carried for him for so many years by God's grace.

We've been reading the Bible together every day ever since. Eventually, it opened up a future for us we never thought possible. But more on that later.

Learning to Dance with God

While everyone else traveled to Switzerland for the convention, Fred and I flew to Rome to begin our thirty-day tour of Europe. We were sad to be parting and would have preferred to stay with the group, but our trip to Rome had already been booked, accommodations already paid for. When we got to Rome, we ran into a bit of a problem: From the start of our trip, we were spending money like it was going out of style, and now we were just about out of traveler's checks. One of the first things we had to do in Rome was run to the American Express to order more checks.

"I can order the checks for you," the agent told us, "but they won't arrive before your next flight to Zurich."

"Pushing back our next flight is out of the question," we said. "First of all, we don't have the money to do that, and second, that would complicate all of our other flights."

"Tell you what I can do," the agent said, "I can have them mail the checks to you in Zurich instead. That seems to be your only option."

We flew into Zurich the following Saturday morning. The American Express, which by now had our checks, closed early on

Saturdays and wouldn't be open again until Monday morning, so unless we wanted to beg for food for the next couple of days, we had to make it in time before it closed. Fortunately, we did.

To our surprise, Merlin and his wife, Ynez, still in town for the convention, walked into the American Express. Instantly, I knew this was a God thing, a divine encounter.

"I can't believe we're running into each other like this," Merlin said. "How was Rome?"

We told him it was sort of disappointing because of our current money situation.

"That's too bad," he said. "Well, I know what will cheer you up: This is the last night of the convention. You gotta come!"

"What do you say?" I said to Fred.

"Let's do it!"

Funny how it worked out that way, I thought later. We had sort of been running from this event, Jonah style, only to find ourselves there anyway.

After dinner with Merlin and Ynez, we arrived at the meeting a little late. The place was packed and alive with God's presence. Eighteen different countries were represented. During the meeting, the primary message was about the Holy Spirit's role in empowering us to preach the gospel to the whole world. As one speaker eloquently put it: "Unfortunately, in Christian history the Holy Spirit has often taken the backseat. For many, the Holy Spirit is the awkward 'third wheel' of the Trinity no one really wants to talk about; sometimes he's forgotten about or ignored altogether. But Jesus physically left our world so that he could send us the Comforter, which should tell us just how important the Holy Spirit is for the church and for each and every one of us. Christ died in our place on a cross and then ascended to heaven so that we could live empowered by the Holy Spirit. The Holy Spirit is essential! He is God. Without him, Christ could not be revealed to us."

He went on to share a whole teaching on the person of the Holy Spirit and the importance of each of the nine gifts of the Spirit, which can be *very* controversial even in the church world. However, this Full Gospel Business Men's group strongly believed in the gifts of the Holy Spirit, including prophesy, healing, and the importance of a supernatural prayer language—"speaking in tongues."

Listening, I thought about my own prayer life. Everything the speaker was saying I could attest to. I started praying in tongues soon after I married Fred. At first there was a bit of hesitation and confusion. *How do I do this? How does it work? Is this really real?* People prayed for me to receive the Holy Spirit and the gift of tongues, but I was still too timid and unsure to speak out and try, even when alone. Then one day during my devotional, while I was reading the story of the day of Pentecost, I suddenly began praying in the Spirit! It was totally by inspiration: In that moment the Holy Spirit came over me—a true divine encounter—and it was like I couldn't help but pray in tongues. The prayers were pouring out of my mouth like an overflowing fountain. I never questioned the truthfulness of tongues again after that.

Throughout the message, I also thought about Fred. I had known and believed all of this for years . . . but what did Fred think? Was he more open to it now? Did it make any sense? This was a brand-new world for me with my Fred.

The preacher closed his message with an altar call: "The baptism of the Holy Spirit is a kind of second work of grace, a second impartation of God upon the believer for his or her empowerment in the kingdom of God to live a Christ-like life. One of the ways this is accomplished is through the gift of tongues, which, as is attested to many times in the New Testament, accompanies the baptism of the Holy Spirit. So I invite you: Those who want to accept Jesus as your Lord and Savior and receive eternal life, come forward. And those of you who want to be baptized in the Holy Spirit, you may also come forward."

Knowing Fred, I really didn't think he would go up. Was I wrong! He was the first to stand and walk up to the stage! I couldn't believe it. I was so proud of him.

The group that had gathered were then led offstage into a separate room for prayer. Fred was in there for an hour.

When he finally came back out, I asked him, "So, what happened?" He told me several people prayed for him, and some pretty "high up there" people at that, like the president of the FGBM and an Episcopal priest.

"Did you speak in tongues?" I asked.

"No," he responded. "But I did have this sensation: My mouth and chin started chattering uncontrollably—but I wasn't cold. I just couldn't speak. Even if I had wanted to say something, anything, even in English, I couldn't, because I just kept chattering uncontrollably. *Something* was happening to me."

Isaiah 28:11 says, "With a stammering lip and an unknown tongue will I speak to these people." I think Fred experienced something like that. He might not have spoken in tongues that night, but by the sound of it, God was working on him in his own way, in his own time.

Watching Fred grow those first few weeks was like watching a flower bloom, a flower I had been waiting to see bloom for a very long time. It was almost as if God had me wait so long to see it, because he knew the longer I waited, the more beautiful and the more vibrant the flower would look to me.

At one point during this time it hit me: Linda's prophecy! I couldn't believe I had forgotten about it. It had been exactly one year since my daughter had been given that prophecy in Tulsa, the one about Fred coming to the Lord in one year's time. When that dawned on me, I broke down and wept. I was so thankful, so full of joy, so in awe of God! I also felt ashamed for my lack of faith. *Why had I doubted? I had no reason not to believe in God's promise.* But I had doubted, and I knew I needed to repent. God's love and grace is so good, so sweet, because the fruit of my repentance only made me more thankful; God had remained faithful to his word despite my faithlessness. You can always count on him!

So much grace in this life, grace every which way we turn. Grace for Fred. Grace for me. Grace for my daughter. Grace before, during, and after the trip. There was nowhere I could turn and not find God's love and provision. The whole thing with Fred was like a big jigsaw puzzle, and each time a piece was put in its proper place, that was grace on grace. No matter what we've done, no matter how far or how long we've run from him, God wants to put the pieces of our lives back together. He ultimately wants us to be at peace, which can only happen when he is the centerpiece of our lives. He *is* Peace! You can't have peace if you don't know Peace. Jesus is the Prince of Peace!

If Fred's grace was also for my benefit (I needed more faith in God), then by that logic whatever measure of grace I had received would be for someone else's benefit too. Grace never stops, never tires. Grace is never done with you. It always wants to bless the next person *through you*. We can never be too thankful; we can never become too loving. Grace captures you so that you become a channel of grace for others.

It's like God is teaching us all how to dance—how to dance with him, how to dance with one another, how we can all dance together in his kingdom! The dance we dance into eternity. The dance that saves our souls, that saves the world. I think that's such a beautiful image: The way out of hell is learning to dance with God, which he leads. When we try to lead the dance—disaster! But when God leads—grace, mercy, hope, love, faith, beauty, truth. The heavenly list goes on and on.

Fred had a long way to go in this dance. But when you think about it, his journey into the grace of God was no closer to its end than mine. How can you compare one person's growth into the

Infinite to another? We'll always need more Grace, more Love, more of his Spirit! Our capacity for him is determined by our capacity to let go and trust in him *for everything!* When we do this, his dance and our dance are one. Thank you, Holy Spirit! Praise you, Jesus!

Nine
Coming Home

Fred:

WHEN WE LANDED in Norway, where my father's side of the family was from, we only had a couple more countries left on the docket before we flew back to California. Once again, by "chance," we ran into a couple from our FGBM group—this time Al and Edith Konsmo, the other younger couple. Ruth and I happened to be staying in the same hotel in Oslo as they were. We said, "Let's team up! Let's see Norway together!" So we rented one car for the four of us and pretty much did everything as a group. Every night, after a long day of sightseeing, we ended by praying together in one of our hotel rooms.

The Konsmos had been steadfastly praying for me during the trip, from the beginning. Like everyone else in our group, they were so overjoyed that I had finally come around to God, but they also knew the work—God's work—wasn't over with me; the battle wasn't over. What kind of soil in my heart did God's word fall on? In other words, the Konsmos felt responsible in helping make sure it was well-tilled, nutrient-rich soil that God's word took root in. Otherwise, there would be no fruit, right? So we prayed every night; they were wonderful times, very encouraging.

But on our last night in Norway, during our nightly prayer session, I could hardly focus. My mind was preoccupied over what I was going to say to my friends back home, and I was really beating myself up over it. "Looks like Fred finally got religion," I could hear them say. Or worse, "Ruth finally wore him down." The problem was I couldn't think of a way to tell my story without making it sound like I lost the war to religion by way of attrition. Nor could I stand the thought of my friends thinking I was doing this whole religion thing just to please someone else or to get my wife off my back—to be cast in that kind of light was anathema to me.

We had about a week of travel left and then it was back to the grind, back to reality. Not only that, this was our last night with the Konsmos. Being with them, praying with them every night, had been a source of strength. It had also helped take my mind off of the inevitable. But now that that source of strength was about to end, I was afraid. It would be Ruth and me again—not that Ruth wasn't also an indispensable source of spiritual strength at that time (and still is), but I needed all the support I could get! Thinking about my life in California, about my work, all of the demands—would I be able to do it? It was relatively easy being a Christian when you were essentially globetrotting with a bunch of people who wanted the best for you in your walk with the Lord. Could I follow Jesus without all that?

One lesson I learned rather quickly, one many of us learn quickly as Christians, was that just because you've met the living Jesus, just because you've been "saved," doesn't mean that the sin in your life magically disappears: "You can't clean a fish until it's been caught" is what I like to say. At the root of all my anxiety was pride. In other words, I didn't want to look stupid in front of my friends. Now, this was only one side of my sinful nature that I was becoming more aware of. I had a lot that still needed cleaning up in my life: fear, anger, bad habits, etc. It was a good thing Christ died for my sins, because I had a lot of them, and without his strength I was powerless against them. It was a good thing God surrounded me with so many loving, supportive, "fanatical" Christians from the very start, because they taught me and, more importantly, modeled what it was like to live under grace.

Getting back to the prayer meeting: It was Edith suddenly speaking in tongues that jolted me back to the present; I was still getting used to people praying like this. When Edith finished, it was silent for a moment. Then, still under the inspiration of the Holy

Spirit, she gave the interpretation herself: "My son, take no thought of what you shall say or what you shall do, but when the time comes, if you will open your mouth to speak, I will fill it."

I was *really* awake now. The words pierced me to my core. There was no questioning that God was addressing this message *to me* through Edith. (It's very easy to forget that God "hears" our thoughts just as well as he hears our spoken words.) God had heard my cry, and he had answered. Of course, as far as I knew, no one else knew this word was specifically for me; I hadn't even confided in Ruth about my worries. But *God knew*, and that's all that mattered. I was humbled, exposed, a little frightened, but mostly deeply reassured.

I made a secret covenant with the Lord right then and there: "Okay, God, if you will be faithful to fill my mouth with what to say, I will do my best to be faithful to open it when the time comes." I thought that was a reasonable enough agreement on my end; I could handle that.

After that night, having heard from God pretty much directly, most of my anxiety dissipated, but I knew I wasn't out of the woods yet. I still had my part to do when the time came. Good feelings weren't going to be enough to get me by; I would have to be obedient, whether I felt like it or not, and then trust God to do the rest. God wasn't going to force my mouth open. He's not in the business of coercion; he's in the business of love, and love requires consent.

Little did I know my first test was right around the corner. When I got back to California, before I even went to my own office, I stopped by to catch up with an old friend of mine, John McInnis.

"Fred! Come on in," John said to me. "I want to hear all about the Holy Land."

John was a local printer I'd been good friends with for many years. We were business colleagues and fishing buddies. He was once the president of the chamber of commerce in Orange and had also been chairman of the planning commission. On top of that, he had gone through all the chairs in the Masonic Lodge. As a well-respected and well-connected businessman about town, John and I ran in many of the same social circles, which was how we met.

John was probably the most "religious" of my friends, but he was by no means devout or even that spiritual, as far as I could tell. Churchgoing seemed to be the extent of his spiritual life—and that was more obligatory than anything else. He lived "like hell" like the rest of us, so hearing his interest in the Holy Land caught me by surprise.

I gave John the bullet-point version of my trip: We did *this*, we saw *that*. Kept it pretty superficial. I talked about Israel, but I didn't go into any great detail about what I was going through at that time and definitely didn't describe what had happened to me in the garden.

When I finished, John said something else I wasn't expecting. He leaned in close and asked, "Now, Fred, after seeing all this, what has this done in your life?" Just like that, a lightbulb switched on in my head. I wasn't sure what John meant by the question, but it was enough to remind me of my promise to God. "This is it," the Holy Spirit whispered to me. "Time to open your mouth." So I did.

Starting from day one of the trip, I told John all about the spiritual struggles I went through: About my initial misgivings beginning that night in Tokyo; how I almost abandoned Ruth in Singapore; about my aversion to all the religious traditions I encountered along the way; about the Church of the Holy Sepulchre and the Church of All Nations. Finally, I got to the part about the Garden Tomb and how God met me there, and how my life was changed as I came to the realization that Christianity wasn't about rules and man's traditions, but about being in a relationship with Christ himself.

I must've been talking for over an hour. John just listened, and I had no idea if I was making any sense. *I probably sound crazy*, I thought.

But the first word out of John's mouth after I finished was, "Amazing," surprising me once again.

Interestingly, I was thinking of the same word, but for a different reason. I was *amazed* that I had shared the gospel with such ease and clarity. At first I had resisted—which is why I think God graciously nudged me in the right direction through John's follow-up question; but once I got going, I was shocked by how naturally the words flowed out of my mouth. "If you open your mouth, I will fill it," God had promised. And his promise came true! If I could've gone back in time to Norway and told myself that in just a couple of weeks I would be confidently sharing the gospel, and with success, I would have announced to God, "You've got the wrong guy."

However, I left John's office on cloud nine—on a heavenly cloud, you could say. I had stepped out in faith, and God had met me there. I felt the rest of the fear and anxiety leave my body. It all seemed laughable to me now; my fear was gone.

When I walked into my own office a little later, the phone was already ringing. My secretary, who I hadn't seen in months, answered and then said, "I don't know how this person knew you'd be in your office at this very moment . . . but it's for you."

Who could it be? Well, it was John McInnes.

"I know we just talked," he said, "but could you share your story again, perhaps tonight over dinner? My wife has to hear about it."

It was like God was telling me, "Now that you *get it*, do it again."

"Sure!" I said.

I brought Ruth with me. For two hours straight I shared my story. I didn't even touch my food once, which went cold long before I was done sharing. No one else got a word in. I was filled with a boldness and a joy I never knew was possible, not to mention sheer endurance: Combined with all the talking I did at John's office earlier that day, I had never talked so much in my entire life! The strange thing was I could've kept going!

God must've really been pleased with my little bit of faithfulness, because soon enough I hardly had to do any of the sharing myself. John McInnis and his wife were so impressed and moved by my story, they started sharing it with everyone they knew. And because they were, like I said, very well-connected and liked in the community, my story spread like wildfire. I had acquaintances and friends coming up to me out of the blue, asking, "Is this true what we've heard about you?"

"It's all true," I'd say.

Then doors started opening up for me to share more broadly. I shared on the Christian Business Men's Connection (CBMC) and at many FGBM events. I was a bit of a local sensation, which was beyond anything I imagined happening.

Meanwhile, I was going to church. Ruth and I were attending the Assemblies of God church in Santa Ana, where Ruth was a Sunday school teacher for the teens. Ruth was one happy camper. For the first time, she could count on her husband going to church with the rest of the family. Also for the first time, there was someone in the family more excited about going to church other than herself—me. It was like a veil had been torn from my eyes. Where before I only saw the grayness and staleness of dead-end religion, full of judgmental hypocrites and the superstitious, now I saw the brightness and beauty of Christ in others: people forgiven and wanting to be near God, just like me.

Everything was going great. Then a few weeks later I received a call from the pastor: "We need to talk," he said.

When we got together, the pastor told us, "As happy as we are for you, Fred, for what God has done for you, we see that you're still smoking. This is a problem. We can't have you in this church if you're going to continue smoking—I'm sorry. Your wife is a youth teacher, and we don't want to be sending the wrong message to our kids. I hope you understand."

It was true, I was still smoking. I knew many believed that disqualified me as a Christian. But for me, smoking wasn't as simple as choosing not to do it: It was an addiction, a nasty habit I had picked up when I was an impressionable kid. For years Ruth had tried getting me to quit, but no matter how hard I tried, it only made the addiction worse, as if it were some angry spirit that only grew angrier and demanded more from me the more I fought it. I was helpless to stop.

Back in Israel, when Ruth and I first started reading the Bible together, we began with Matthew, going verse by verse. A few days into our readings we came to the verse that says, "It's not what you take into the body that defiles the body, but it's what comes out of the heart." This verse really stood out to me because it reaffirmed what the Holy Spirit had told me in the Garden Tomb: that we come to the Lord and accept his free gift of salvation *as we are*, that he accepted me as I was. Hearing this had healed something in me much worse than my smoking addiction: my hard heart!

Seeing this confirmed in Scripture was also a big deal because it illustrated that God could speak to me personally through his Word. God wasn't just someone who only existed in church somewhere, or in heaven out there, but he existed in our homes, in our hearts, and in the Bible sitting on the shelf, just waiting to be opened. This was the God who *speaks*, who was always speaking, and who desired to speak to each and every one of us at all times. I could go to God himself with my problems and my questions, and I could hear directly from him.

I wanted to tell my pastor that God was more concerned with the condition of my heart and the kind of "works and words" that came out of it, that as unhealthy as it was, my smoking habit didn't disqualify me from being in a relationship with God. Thankfully, I realized, before it was too late, that I would have said this defensively, in a spirit of pride. The conversation could have easily turned ugly had I went in that direction, but by God's grace, I understood the point my pastor was making, as much as it hurt to hear him say it. I didn't want to be a bad influence on anyone, especially kids.

"We understand," I said. "We're grateful for the time we've had in your church." And I meant it.

I guess the only good thing about getting kicked out of your church is that it frees you to look for a new one. Some friends of ours, Spirit-filled Episcopalians—which initially I thought was kind of odd, almost oxymoronic—invited us to their church. Turns out this too was another divine encounter.

One of the first differences between Episcopalians and Pentecostals that I learned about was that there were no rules forbidding you to smoke or drink. In fact, there is a common saying among Episcopalians: "When three or four Episcopalians get together, there's always a fifth!"—referring to liquor. Well, that was music to my ears; I didn't have to be someone I wasn't.

Now, these were the early days of the charismatic renewal blossoming in the Episcopal Church. God was really pouring out his Spirit on them in a way the Episcopalians had never seen before, or since. It all started with a man named Dennis J. Bennett, an Episcopal priest at a church in Van Nuys, California. On April 3, 1960, Bennett shocked his congregation when he told them he had been personally baptized in the Holy Spirit accompanied with the gift of speaking in tongues. He then went on to say that he wasn't anyone special, that the baptism of the Holy Spirit, God's second impartation for believers, was for everyone. Bennett was subsequently forced to resign from his post and moved to Seattle, where he began pastoring again. *Time* magazine and *Newsweek* picked up his story, making him into an instant international sensation and controversial figure.

Ruth and I joined an Episcopal church just a year after this had all gone down. We also joined a Spirit-filled, Spirit-led Episcopalian prayer group, which were popping up everywhere, it seemed. All of these spiritual shakeups and new directions were very intriguing and exciting, and as onlookers at the time, we were watching with great anticipation to see just how far into mainstream Christianity the charismatic renewal would go.

Frustratingly, however, I still hadn't been baptized in the Holy Spirit; I still hadn't been granted the gift of speaking in tongues. Now, I would never say that Christians who don't speak in tongues aren't Christians, nor would I say that they don't have the Spirit in some measure for themselves. But biblically speaking, whenever the apostles laid hands on people to receive the Holy Spirit, the evidence of the authentic indwelling of the Spirit was always that they spoke in tongues, beginning with Pentecost itself.

The Scriptures say that the gift is available to everyone if they want it: "For the promise is unto you," speaking of the Holy Spirit, "and to your children, and to all that are afar off, even as many as the LORD our God shall call."[2] In other words, if the Holy Spirit is available to everyone, then the gift of tongues is available to everyone. This connection was important for me to understand when it came to understanding the purpose of speaking in tongues. In 1 Corinthians 14, Paul lays out the value and purpose for praying in the Spirit, or speaking in tongues. The significance is that you're speaking in a language initiated by the Holy Spirit for intercession and edification. It's God praying *through you* to achieve *his* purposes: "*Your* kingdom come, *your* will be done." If that is, in a nutshell, the true significance of tongues, then why wouldn't I want that for myself?

Around this time, Ruth and I went to a big Christian meeting where David du Plessis was guest speaking. This turned out to be another significant divine encounter. David was from South Africa and used powerfully by God to bring the charismatic renewal to many of the historic churches. In fact, he was invited to the World Council of Churches one year to share on the baptism of the Holy Spirit. Some of his people criticized him for agreeing to meet with the more liberally minded churches, but David truly made an impact while he was there, essentially opening up the discussion of the Holy Spirit to a much larger audience in the traditional Christian world. Up until that time, Pentecostals were perceived as uneducated, strange, and not really part of the church. But David, being a scholar himself and, more importantly, anointed, helped change that image for a lot of mainstream Christians, which was how he became known as "Mr. Pentecost."

After the meeting, I went up for prayer. I thought if anyone could confer the Holy Spirit to me, it was this man. But just as in Zurich, the same stammering sensation came over me, but no tongues. I'll admit, I was a little disappointed going home that night.

The next morning, however, something strange happened. I woke up and . . . wasn't craving tobacco whatsoever! I couldn't remember the last time that had happened. I didn't put a whole lot of thought into it right away, but as the hours passed, I noted that the craving still hadn't returned. *What is going on*? Amazingly, by the end of the day, I hadn't smoked my pipe at all, nor had I felt an iota of craving to do so. What did it mean? In all my years as a smoker, I had never experienced this. I had tried quitting so many times before, always fighting tooth and nail to resist. In the end I always lost. Sometimes out of desperation I'd throw my pipe in the trash, but then Ruth, graciously knowing I'd be needing it a little later, would secretly retrieve it. On this day, though, there was no need to fight.

"When was the last time you smoked?" Ruth asked me.

"Right before last night's meeting," I answered.

Then it hit me: When David prayed for me, God may not have given me the gift of tongues, but he did heal me of my smoking addiction! There was no other explanation. The next day I didn't smoke either, or the next, or the next. Truth be told, I had cravings, but the Holy Spirit delivered me. It was a total healing, a divine encounter.

What an amazing God we have! He knows our needs better than we know them ourselves. His plans and his ways are so much better, so much wiser than our own. I can't describe enough how liberating it was to be free of my addiction. I can't say why God healed me of my smoking instantaneously that night, since I hadn't even asked for it, but I can say with confidence that God is good and far more patient with me than I am with him. And he wants to heal your addictions too! Whatever they may be. Now, it might not happen the way it happened for me. (It seems like God never quite performs the same miracle in the same way twice.) But no matter how it happens, when you encounter God, you will experience freedom. You can be assured that God is for your *total* restoration—in him.

After being healed from smoking, I wasn't too worried that God hadn't granted me the gift of tongues; I had other people worrying for me.

"Are you speaking in tongues yet?" an Episcopal friend of mine asked me one day when he stopped by my office.

I didn't know how to answer. "I'm doing all that I can," I finally said. "It's not like I haven't tried." Apparently, my answer wasn't good enough, because my friend kept insisting I do more.

"Have you *tried* speaking in tongues?" he asked.

"No."

"Well, maybe you should try. See what happens."

I was getting frustrated. I wanted to tell him, "Okay, I got it! I'll try harder. Now can you please leave me to my work?" Yet something about my friend's sincerity and pesky persistence kept me quiet (mostly), and it stuck with me for the rest of the day. So much so that on my drive home from work I decided to take my friend's advice and give tongues the good ol' college try. I had a couple of little sounds stored in my head—I guess you could call them syllables—that I thought I had picked up from listening to other people speaking in tongues. Not knowing how else to begin, I began uttering those two rudimentary sounds. I felt like a kid learning how to speak for the first time; I didn't know what I was doing.

As I drove through Orange and "prayed," the spiritual breakthrough I was hoping for never came. More than anything, I felt silly, like a bad actor. *Get him off the stage already!*

I kept repeating and repeating those same syllables, praying under my breath, as though I had a tune stuck in my head. Even as I lay in bed, falling asleep, I was still muttering those two little sounds, still struggling with myself.

When I woke up the next morning, Ruth was staring at me strangely.

"What is it?" I asked, half awake.

"You were speaking in tongues in your sleep last night," she said.

"I was?"

"You were."

"Are you sure? Maybe you were dreaming that I did."

"I'm sure, Fred. Your praying woke me up. I think God baptized you in the Holy Spirit while you were sleeping!"

The whole morning I pondered what this meant. I had never heard of someone being baptized in the Holy Spirit in their sleep. *How does that work? Do I really have the gift?* The first chance I got I put it to the test. When I started praying in tongues this time, it wasn't those same two basic sounds I was turning over and over; it was something else, something supernatural. I was praying in the Spirit! To be clear: I was doing the speaking (God wasn't controlling me), but the Spirit was giving the utterance, which is where the power comes from. In this state, I could consciously decide, "Okay, now I will begin praying in the Spirit and rely on the Holy Spirit to transform my mere words into heavenly speech."

Before, I had assumed the Holy Spirit would do all the work for me, sort of just, you know, squeeze it out of me when the time came. That's why I was somewhat reluctant to even give it a try; I thought I just needed to sit back and wait for it to happen. But that's not how it works, which was what my Episcopalian friend was trying to tell me: "You just have to yield to it." Even though it was my very own lips, my tongue, and my voice that I had to offer, I still had to open my mouth, in faith, in order to receive that gift. And, well, that takes some initiative on our part.

Over the years, I've thought about why God baptized me in the Holy Spirit during my sleep. I can only speculate. When I was awake, I wasn't fully submitting my mind to God. In other words, I was trying too hard, thinking too rationally. I thought I could make it happen through sheer effort. But once I fell asleep, my conscious, rational mind was no longer in control, allowing the Holy Spirit to begin speaking *through me*. "The spirit is willing, but the flesh is weak."[3] Before, when I was trying to speak in tongues, my spirit was definitely willing, but I was trying to do it under my own power rather than submitting my weakness, my inability, to God. As I slept, my spirit was free to commune with *the* Spirit, and he manifested his power, giving his free *gift*, in my weakness.

I also think God answered my prayer in my sleep to say that he does the giving and he gives in his own time, honoring our requests through the Holy Spirit. There was no way I could *earn* any gift of God for myself—otherwise it wouldn't be a gift! At the same time, I believe God was pleased with my persistence:

> What man is there among you who, if his son asks for bread, will give him a stone? Or if he asks for a fish, will give him a serpent? If you then, being evil, know how to give good gifts to your children, how much more will your Father who is in heaven give good things to those who ask Him?[4]

God is the Good Giver. He listens to the requests of his children and honors their asking. Perhaps persistent asking is necessary sometimes to reveal our own motivation: *Do I want this for God's glory, or for mine? Because I want to grow closer to him, or because this is what's expected of me?* We are not always ready for the gift when we begin asking for it. Sometimes God uses our asking to prepare our hearts, to humble us, to make us ready to receive what we ask for.

Whatever the case may be, having woken up with a whole new prayer language was like waking up on Christmas morning! I've been speaking in tongues ever since. It not only changed my prayer life, it changed my whole life. From then on, I was living in greater trust to God, empowered by the Spirit like never before.

Ten

The Afterglow and the Ichthys

Ruth:

NOT LONG AFTER Fred and I got back from our trip, we started a Bible study at our home in Orange. For us, the study was a natural extension of our own daily readings of the Scriptures that we began doing together in Israel. As Fred had discovered, if the Bible was one of the primary ways God spoke to us, why would we only read it once in a while or only when we were in church?

The McInneses were some of the first to regularly attend our Bible study, but pretty soon thirty to forty-five people were coming every week. We made it a point not to bring in a regular teacher or pastor. We didn't want the study to be church in the traditional sense, and we certainly didn't want anyone to replace their Sunday morning service with it, including ourselves.

Doing our study this particular way was quite freeing, actually. Instead of having a speaker talk to our group for a half hour from a pulpit, we could be more exploratory and open, with everyone participating. From time to time we did bring in guest speakers to help with a particular chapter or passage in the Bible, but it wasn't the norm, and it wasn't why people came. People came to discover God's Word for themselves, to ask questions, to pray. We started in Matthew (as Fred and I had done before) and went verse by verse, taking as much time as was needed with each verse for it to really sink in. We stuck to that format: It took us ten years to read and study through the whole New Testament. Ten years!

Now, you might be thinking there isn't anything special about what we were doing. Today it seems like you can find any style of Bible study imaginable. But the way we were doing it back in the early sixties was brand new and really exciting. The Bible was truly coming alive for us—some for the first time! People from all kinds of Christian backgrounds were showing up. Non-Christians too.

We kept it as informal and homey as possible. I served dessert every week. There was no membership requirement. You didn't have to look a certain way. Fred said he wanted the Bible study to be like the garden: natural, diverse, open. He wanted people to come meet God *as they were*, as he had in Jerusalem. God would do the rest from there; God would clean us up if we let him.

And he did! People were getting saved, miracles were happening, people were getting baptized in the Holy Spirit. It became more than just a Bible study: It became a sacred time devoted to the experience of God, to divine encounters, whether through his Word, outreach, music, prayer, or a meal. We wanted it all—and more!

Literally, we wanted more. We met on Tuesday evenings, so we couldn't expect people to stay too late into the night; but neither did we want to quench the Spirit. The study itself went for about an hour and a half, and then we'd have dessert and some fellowship as a kind of intermission so that if people had to leave, they could feel comfortable doing so. But most stayed for the "afterglow," or what we also called "sharing time." I'm not sure where we got the term *afterglow* from, but I certainly hadn't heard of one until we started having them. The afterglow was sort of like the afterparty of Bible studies, where things got a little more intense, a little more unpredictable and off-script. We mainly used this time to pray for people, since there wasn't enough time during the studying portion of the meeting to do that; we wanted a time where we could invite the Spirit and let him move and flow as he wished. Another reason we formatted it like this was so that we didn't scare newcomers or nonbelievers.

Most afterglows lasted well into the night, way past everybody's bedtimes. Sometimes we'd look at the clock and suddenly realize it was the next day! That's how much the Spirit would be moving on any given night. Just about anything happened: healings, Holy

Ghost baptisms, exorcisms, prophecies, words of knowledge, speaking in tongues, you name it. In this sense, it wasn't *just* a time for prayer, but also a time where people were free to exercise their spiritual giftings or to ask for the gifts.

By the time it was all over, we were usually all pretty exhausted, but we were also on a spiritual high from hours of prayer and worship. It's hard to describe. We were drunk in the Spirit but also ready for bed. Anyway, people would stream out of our house around midnight, sometimes later, laughing, saying goodbye, shutting car doors, starting up engines; their exits were generally pretty loud. Too loud, actually.

One night, as everyone was leaving, we noticed a bright light coming from our next-door neighbors' bedroom window and a sign that said, "Quiet! Light sleepers!" *Uh oh,* I thought. Suddenly I was able to hear just how loud we were being! My heart sank. I felt like the worst neighbor in the world. These were our friends—Jack and Marie! Before Fred and I went on our trip across the world, Fred and Jack would often work on their boats together on Sunday mornings while the kids and I were away at church. We'd also go on family trips with them to the river, fishing and waterskiing and that sort of thing.

But ever since we'd gotten back, with Fred going to church and having this Bible study, we didn't see much of Jack and Marie anymore or go out of our way to spend time with them. And now *this*: We'd been keeping them up every Tuesday night for who knows how long! What kind of Christian witness was that? I felt horrible.

The following Bible study we did our best to keep the noise to a minimum; we tried wrapping things up earlier too. I guess our best efforts weren't enough, because this time the sign in the window was written in a threatening red! *Oh dear! What are we to do? How do we make this right?*

As though it couldn't get any worse, their dog was poisoned a few weeks later and died. *They're going to think we did it!* I thought frightfully. Of course, we would never even think of doing such a thing, but from their point of view, I could see how it might look that way, though they never went out and actually said so to our face. After this happened, we were determined more than ever to repair the relationship. *We can't let it continue like this.* We prayed that God would do some kind of miracle.

Our only remaining form of communication with them was with Marie, who worked as a teller where we banked. Whenever Fred had business at the bank and Marie happened to be working, he'd purposefully stand in her queue even if it meant waiting longer. One day during this rift, Fred did exactly that.

"Hi, Marie. How are you doing?" Fred said when he got to the front of the line.

"Oh, Fred! Did you hear what happened?" she said, visibly upset.

"No. What happened?"

"Jack's brother died of a heart attack!"

"Oh no! I'm so sorry, Marie. When did this happen?"

Marie, crying, said, "Just this past week. Jack is just beside himself. He doesn't know what to do. I'm really worried for him."

"Jack needs the peace only the Lord can give him," Fred said, going out on a limb.

"I know," Marie replied dolefully before weeping uncontrollably.

Fred turned around: There was a long line of confused customers behind him, waiting to be seen, wondering (I can only guess) what Fred had done to make their teller cry in the middle of the bank.

When Fred was able to calm her down, he said, "You know, we're having our Bible study tonight. Why don't you and Jack come? We have a sharing time. We can pray for you and Jack. I think you'll find that it helps."

"That sounds like a good idea," Marie answered. "Could you come over later today and invite Jack? He might go if you ask him personally."

"Sure thing, Marie."

The first thing Fred said to me when he got home was, "You won't believe what just happened!" He then explained everything. Amazed by what I was hearing, I then said, "Well, *you* won't believe this: The mailman left Jack and Marie's mail in our mailbox today! I haven't taken it over to them yet. That's the perfect excuse to go over there and invite Jack, don't you think?" *This is the miracle we've been looking for*, I thought. *Another divine encounter.*

I think Fred was still dealing with some pride or fear in his heart, because he asked me if I would go instead, which I did gladly. This was all God's plan anyway. I knocked on Jack's door, gave him his mail, and then invited him to Bible study. It didn't surprise me one bit when Jack agreed to come that night. I was so excited and full of faith on that short walk from their porch to mine! I couldn't wait to pray for them and tell them more about what God wanted for their lives—healing, peace, and eternal life!

Of course, the plans we devise are rarely God's plans. They only stayed for the first half of the meeting and then left after dessert. Not only did I not get the chance to share with them, I didn't even get the chance to ask them what they had thought of the meeting. But what I feared was a missed opportunity turned out to be exactly what Jack and Marie needed. So often we try to rush things; we have to remember that seeds need time. In the parable of the sower, it's the seed that falls on rocky ground and springs up immediately that doesn't last.

To our surprise, Jack and Marie showed up the next Tuesday night. Marie approached me before things got going and asked, "If Jack and I stay for the sharing time, could we share something with the whole group?"

"Of course!" I said. "We'd love that."

What could she possibly want to share? I wondered the whole first half of the meeting.

When the time came, Marie stood up and said, "We just wanted to tell you all that Jack and I were baptized last Saturday night."

What? Baptized? We never even had the chance to get them born again, I thought with a little frustration. Not that this wasn't great news—I was happy for them but a little confused.

Marie went on to say that on the previous Wednesday, some Baptist friends of theirs came to visit them. A few days later Jack and Marie joined them at a Baptist Bible study, where they got to talking how much they had enjoyed their experience at our Bible study. Being the good Baptists they were, their friends asked Jack and Marie if they would like to commit their lives to Christ and know him personally.

"Yes, we would."

Their friends wasted no time after that and led them in the Sinner's Prayer. Then they asked, "Why don't we take you to our church right now and baptize you? You need to be baptized."

"Sounds great!"

So they went from estranged, unbelieving neighbors to saved and baptized in Christ, with our relationship fully restored and made stronger through Christ, all in less than one week! What a glorious turn of events!

Jack and Marie became regulars at the Bible study from then on. In fact, they stayed after and joined the afterglow. Jack even brought his guitar and took part in the worship time. To see the tangible transformation in their lives now that they were saved by grace was such a joy. It's true what Jesus said: Some do the planting, and some do the watering, but it's God who does the growing. Jack and Marie were living examples of that beautiful truth. We all are!

Sadly, Jack died a few years later from a heart attack, just as his brother had. We mourned his death, but not like the world mourns death. We knew he was more alive than he was before, more alive than we were then and are now. We had the comfort of knowing we would see him again. His death was bittersweet, but in Christ the sweet always wins in the end.

Another significant story during our Bible study period was our involvement—well, mostly Fred's involvement—with the commercial development of the sign of the fish. To tell that story, though, I need to back up a little bit and share Fred's connections with Oral Roberts and Dr. Bob Frost.

Not long after we had returned from our trip, Fred came across an ad in a paper that said, "If you're interested in a deeper life in the Spirit, come to Christian Center in Anaheim." Christian Center, later known as Melodyland Christian Center, was a small up-and-coming church. Ralph Wilkerson was the pastor. We decided to check it out.

The church met on Sunday afternoons at an Assistance League building. (We were also going to Clifton's Cafeteria on Saturday mornings, where the FGBM chapter met, as well as the Episcopal Bible study on Saturday nights; on top of all that, we were doing our own Bible study on Tuesdays. We were pretty busy.) Ralph had a knack for getting incredibly anointed, well-known charismatic Christian evangelists to speak at Christian Center. He was passionate about sharing the reality of the baptism of the Holy Spirit with the world. When Fred went to receive prayer from David du Plessis, for instance, that was at Christian Center. Ralph also had Kathryn Kuhlman come and speak. Ralph was so wonderful. He loved to share the stage; he gave his platform to any preacher he felt was really legitimate and had a good message. In fact, he was greatly responsible for the charismatic renewal in Southern California.

Oral Roberts had a house in Corona del Mar that he stayed at during summers to get away from the Oklahoma heat. And Ralph being Ralph, he got Oral to come speak at Christian Center one Saturday evening, which was when we became acquainted with him.

Before all this, Fred thought Oral was the biggest charlatan in the world, only interested in using religion for profit. That all changed when Fred got to know him.

Fred and Ruth with Oral Roberts (center)

After spending a week or two together traveling around, Oral took Fred to his beach house. There Oral shared how Stanford University had tried to destroy his son's faith, which sparked Oral's vision to establish a Spirit-filled university focused on educating the "whole person"—mind, body, and spirit. This ultimately became the organizing meeting of Oral Roberts University.

Oral asked Fred if he would accept a position on the board of ORU. Fred respectfully declined, explaining that he felt too underqualified, but Oral insisted, saying, "God told me you need to be part of this." Well, who could argue with that, especially coming from someone as anointed and experienced as Oral? Fred took the offer in the end and held that position for seven years.

One of the first tasks the board members were faced with was staffing the university with Spirit-filled professors. This immediately brought to Fred's mind his friend Dr. Bob Frost, whom we had connected with when we took our daughter, Linda, to see if she would possibly want to attend Westmont, a Christian college in Santa Barbara. Having been recently baptized in the Holy Spirit, Dr. Frost had begun teaching his students that the gifts of the Spirit had not ceased in the church after the deaths of the apostles, which he had previously believed, but that the gifts were for *today* and for *everyone*. Well, Westmont was not happy. He was asked to step down from his positions as professor and chair of the Life Science department.

The building of ORU

Fred: "I see the Oral Roberts University as a hub of the Holy Spirit. It is the focal point for the Spirit-filled believers of all faiths. Its potential is so great, it is beyond our human comprehension."

Knowing Dr. Frost was Spirit-filled and in need of a new job, Fred thought ORU would be the perfect fit for him. He flew him out there, and after a brief interview with Oral, Dr. Frost was pretty much hired on the spot. He sort of became the poster boy for what to look for in potential professors.

Dr. Frost worked for ORU for several years. Both he and Fred were there to see the first graduating class walk. But then in 1969 Dr. Frost got kind of crossed up with a colleague, an old-time Pentecostal, and left ORU to take a position elsewhere; Fred also quit the board after seven years of service.

Fred on the ORU Board
(bottom row, third from the right)

Soon after this, Dr. Frost traveled to Minneapolis for a meeting. There he happened to meet a machinist who showed Dr. Frost a little plaque he had made. On it was the sign of the fish design, known as the Ichthys, with "IXOYE" written inside. For reasons I'll explain shortly, Dr. Frost liked the plaque so much, the machinist let him take one with him back to California to give to Fred. Fred also liked it so much, he displayed it on his front door.

Now, if you don't know the meaning of the Ichthys, I'll explain. In early Christian history, during Roman rule, it was illegal to be a Christian. If you were caught disrespecting Caesar or any of the Roman gods, or if you were singled out as a Christian, you could be tortured and even put to death. Early Christians developed a simple but effective way of secretly identifying one another using the Ichthys.

Ichthys means *fish* in Greek, spelled "IXOYE" in Greek letters. From this, early Christians made an acronym that translates to "Jesus Christ, God's Son, Savior." All one had to do was draw a fish and that would tell others what you believed. For example, if back then you met a stranger and wanted to know if he or she was a believer, you could discreetly draw an arc in the dirt with your foot (or wherever it could be drawn); if the other person was also a Christian, he or she would then add a second arc to yours, completing the fish. If the person wasn't a Christian, he'd just think you were doodling in the dirt, or think nothing of it at all.

The Ichthys, often called the "Jesus fish," is pretty much common knowledge today, but back in the early sixties, it wasn't. To the average person it just looked like a bunch of random symbols, and how it related to fish was not self-evident. Fred and I had learned about the Ichthys when we were in Rome; we saw the symbol for the first time inside the city's catacombs.

"What in the world is hanging on your door?" guests would often ask when they came over, most assuming it was a fraternity thing, which didn't seem very consistent with us. This gave us the opportunity to tell the story of the Ichthys. Everyone was so amazed, and our sign became such a conversation piece, that Fred started thinking about how he could begin using the Ichthys in everyday life like the early Christians did.

His answer came a few days later when Fred noticed a car decal advertising auto air conditioning (this was back when air conditioning was an after-market accessory). It then dawned on Fred: *Why don't we do something like that? We could come up with an Ichthys decal for cars so that Christians could identify one another on the road!* Fred took his idea to John McInnis in the printing business, who then took it to an artist he knew, who then came up with a design for the decal. Like our plaque, the original design had the silver fish against a black background with "IXOYE" outlined in black inside the fish.

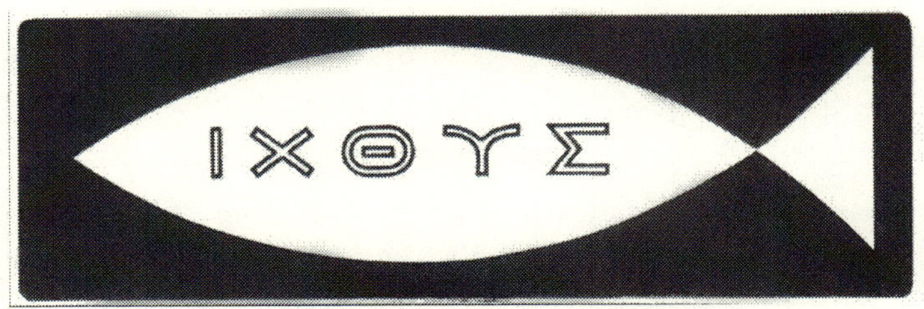

Some Baptist friends of ours, Carl and Thelma Cook, who had recently been baptized in the Holy Spirit, were planning on traveling to Mexico as missionaries. Carl had been praying about developing some kind of mail-order business so they could be self-supporting on the mission field rather than forced to rely on somewhat unreliable outside funds. He just needed a product.

Then Carl saw Fred's decal. He was so excited about it, he asked Fred if he could sell them from Mexico.

"I believe this decal is the answer to my prayers," he said.

Fred wasn't interested in money or recognition, so he gave Carl full rights to the decal: "If this thing helps advance the kingdom, that's all I really care about."

Carl felt like the decal needed an explanation, so the first thing he did was write a blurb to go with it. Part of it said: "Placing this ancient CHRISTIAN SYMBOL on your home, car, office, or other prominent place immediately identifies you as a Christian, and curiosity will force all others to ask what it means—thus giving you the opportunity to witness to them of the Saviour."

Next he went down to the Long Beach public library, pulled out telephone books for all the major cities in America, and looked up every Christian bookstore he could find. One by one he called them all, asking if he could send samples of his decal for potential sale. And would you believe it—it worked! He was able to get a lot of those bookstores to sell the decal at seventy-five cents apiece.

The decal took off like wildfire after that. We started seeing our design all over the place, mostly on the backs of cars. Eventually they became so popular they went around the world. I'm sure you've seen them yourself.

For the first ten years or so it was just our original design on the market—the silver-and-black decal. But then Calvary Chapel picked it up and started making bumper stickers with the tagline "Get Hooked" underneath the fish. This was 1970, the time of Timothy O'Leary and psychedelics. A lot of kids were getting "hooked" on mind-altering drugs. Calvary Chapel wanted to appeal to that crowd: Instead of getting hooked on drugs, they wanted kids to get hooked on Jesus, which I thought was pretty smart of them. Later Calvary Chapel came out with the plastic fish emblem for the car, which also became immensely popular. Some of them had a little cross or "Jesus" inside. These went worldwide too.

It's amazing to think that, in a way, it all started with our front door. We could've made a lot of money, but that was never our goal. "Store up for yourselves treasures in heaven,"[5] Jesus said, and that's how we saw it. Your money doesn't follow you into heaven, nor will the money your children inherit follow them. We leave this world with what is left in our hearts. Will your heart be full of joy, full of hope, full of gratitude, full of light? Will it be a soft heart you die with, the heart of a child? Or will it be dark, fixated on the past, full of fear of what's to come, regretful for having loved so little and for caring too much about what is fleeting and superficial? Fred and I were already blessed beyond our wildest imaginations—blessed in the Lord. What could a few more bucks do? They would amount to nothing more than a drop of water in the sea. Living eternally with our King and Savior Jesus Christ is and *will be* our most glorious reward!

Eleven
Lonnie

Fred:

ONE OF MY big work projects after coming back from our trip was buying growers in Orange County out of their orange groves and then selling them more acreage at cheaper costs in Riverside County (about an hour's drive away). During this process, Ruth and I took a number of trips to the city of Riverside. We thought the area was so beautiful; we loved how open it was. In fact, we loved it so much that in 1962 we bought a large piece of property up in the western hills of Riverside for growing citrus groves of our own. Eventually we would build a house there—our dream house.

By 1965 we thought everything was in place to begin building on our property and moved from Orange to Corona, a neighboring city of Riverside, while we waited. Due to a few unexpected speed bumps along the way, for about three years we lived in a number of rentals in the Riverside/Corona area as we waited to get the go-ahead to begin building. Then in 1968 we finally broke ground, and the following year we officially moved into the Waugh Ranch, where we still live to this day.

We designed the Ranch partly based on our experience renting the three years before. One house we rented was two stories. Well, Ruth really grew to hate hauling things up and down stairs, so a one-story house it would be. In another house, we had a pool outside and a pool table inside. That house was a lot of fun—a little too much fun. Any social gathering we had inevitably ended up at one of those two spots; it was more of a party house than anything else. No pool or pool table, then, or anything else that might distract guests from the chief reason we wanted people over: to experience God.

When we built the Ranch, hosting Bible meetings was in the forefront of our minds. The most important feature we put in, therefore, was the living room, where the meetings would be held. We designed it not only to be big and spacious, but we also lowered it by a couple of steps, which could either be used as additional seating or as a kind of stage for speakers. We also put in dark green carpet throughout the whole house to help with spills and what have you.

Meanwhile, since it was official that we would be moving, we began attending All Saints Episcopal Church in Riverside. Father Bellis, a Spirit-filled priest originally from Garden Grove, whom we had met through mutual friends at our Bible study in Orange, was now the rector at All Saints. Little did we know that God had a number of divine encounters in store and would work through us and amongst us in that church (and in Riverside more broadly) in powerful ways in the years to come—things that wouldn't only reverberate in Southern California, but throughout the world.

The sixties brought about the rise and fall of a myriad of countercultural movements that swept across the world, movements that had in mind the reshaping of preestablished social structures and ruling worldviews. The sexual revolution, the civil rights movement, anti-war and anti-capitalist movements, hippies, drug culture, the rise of feminism and gay rights, to name a few. We think times are turbulent now (and they certainly are), but having lived through the sixties, it's hard to say it was any less chaotic and alarming then than it is today: the assassinations of John F. Kennedy, Robert F. Kennedy, Martin Luther King Jr., and Malcolm X; massive protests that led to rioting and later the death of a number of college students at the hands of the National Guard; disturbing images of brutality and war crimes being pumped into our living room televisions from the Vietnam War. By the late sixties and on into the seventies, it truly felt like the country was being split apart at the seams, that fear and violence were in the air.

It certainly wasn't *all* doom and gloom. Despite his tragic death, Martin Luther King Jr.'s non-violent, largely Christian movement accomplished tremendous good for African Americans and for the country as a whole. And the search for meaning, authenticity, and a true spiritual experience that so much of the American youth was yearning for during that time had plenty of merit and was, in retrospect, good reason to be optimistic—even if that search was undermined by the shedding of conventional sexual mores, its openness to occultism, and the proclivity for drug abuse. Nonetheless, these kids were on to *something!*

Largely speaking, the American church was not as it should have been. For the most part Christianity had become a religion of the past, being deaf or contemptuous of the present, and therefore had no future. There was nothing *radical* about it. The call to "die to self" and "take up one's cross" had been exchanged for the American dream and the strict adherence to theological traditions that seemingly had little to no relevance in real, everyday life, other than showing up for church once a week.

But then, in the late 1960s, all that began to be challenged, beginning with a spirited young hippie named Lonnie Frisbee. Lonnie had prayed to receive Christ as an eight-year-old child, but in his early teens was drawn away by the rebellious anti-establishment spirit that was descending upon all of America. Lonnie and his classmates were among the first to experiment with LSD and would flock to the mountains outside of Palm Springs to Tahquitz Canyon, where they would reportedly do things like strip down, drop LSD, and as they would say, "trip." It was later in this same canyon where Lonnie, at age eighteen, had a vision that changed the trajectory of his life and would touch an entire generation.

Here is an excerpt from Lonnie's autobiography, *Not by Might, Nor by Power: The Jesus Revolution*, about this transformative experience.

Lonnie's Vision

I [Lonnie] felt a destiny surrounding me, but was, at the same time, confused about life and death and even questioned the existence of any particular spiritual reality. Who *really* knew the truth? I remembered from my church background that Jesus claimed to be the truth. I had definitely felt the presence of God when I asked Christ into my life as a child. I also felt his presence at the summer camps, but it still seemed pretty bold for Jesus to say things like, "I am the way, the truth, and the life. No one comes to the Father except through Me," or "I am the good shepherd who lays his life down for the sheep," or "I am the door."[6] (Sorry Jim, but you have *major* competition.) I was definitely confused but very open and honestly seeking. I would wonder, "How does it all fit?"

One day I was up in the canyon again by myself. It was a real hike back on the Tahquitz Canyon trail. There is a beautiful stream and waterfalls along the way, and it is such a cool place. I finally arrived at one of my favorite spots. I took off all my clothes and literally screamed up to heaven, "Jesus, if you are really real—reveal yourself to me!!!"

Suddenly the whole atmosphere began to change around me. It began to tingle and shimmer and glow. I thought, "Uhh–ohhh! I don't even want to be here!" I was scared and shocked, positive it was not an LSD flashback. I didn't hear an audible voice, but I knew that I was in the presence of God Almighty. Then I saw a radiant vision, clear as crystal. I saw thousands and thousands of young people at the ocean lined up in huge crowds along the coast, going out into the water to be baptized. I could see it! I knew instantly that Jesus was real and that he was calling me to follow him. As the Lord lifted up my eyes, I saw a harvest field of people. They were like a huge wheat field. I saw in the vision thousands of people in the valley of decision.

The power of the Holy Spirit surrounded me from within and without. Then I saw a light from heaven come down and ordain me, and I could hear him say, "Go in my name, for I have touched your lips with a coal of fire that burns ever before the presence of God. Proclaim to the people that I am coming soon."

It was the most radical moment of my life. At eighteen years old, I was being called by God to serve him. It blew my mind, but I definitely said, "Yes, Lord!"

I came off that mountain a different person. I still didn't have all the answers, but I knew for sure that Jesus was real. He had responded to my desperate cry. I had an instant revelation of my calling. What a privilege, what a high calling, to be used by a loving God, a God who loved us so much that he died on a cross to save us from destruction, to save us from ourselves. All the scriptures from my childhood started to kick in and take on new meaning with revelation and life. I realized that the written Word of God was true and supernatural. God was invading my life, and it was so powerful and absolutely wonderful. I didn't need drugs anymore!

Back home, my friends and loved ones soon said that I was mad, but I was *struck* and had to obey. I immediately went to the beaches and preached. I would go to the teen dances where I used to go raise hell, and now proclaim that Jesus was Lord and that he was coming back. I could hear the young people my same age laughing and saying, "Let's go out at break time and hear Lonnie talk about God. Did you hear that Lonnie overdosed and had a nervous breakdown?"

As I continued to be faithful, the Lord slowly brought the vision about. One believed, then two, then five, then ten, then there were fifty, and then there were a hundred people coming to know Jesus at every single meeting I preached in. There came a day down the road a little when thousands came to the beach at Corona del Mar to participate in mass baptisms in the ocean, catching the attention of the whole world—*exactly* like the vision I saw.

Hippie Christians

Lonnie is credited with being the main catalyst of the Jesus People movement, which was soon making national and international news at its height from about 1969 through 1973. This huge movement also birthed two modern-day denominations: Calvary Chapel and the Vineyard. Obviously, many other wonderful and very anointed Christian leaders besides Lonnie have played and continue to play key roles in all this history. Many books, major magazines, films, and other media have documented much of Lonnie Frisbee's story as well as the history of the Jesus People movement.

Even though Lonnie walked away from the pernicious sides of the hippie lifestyle, such as using psychedelics and sexual promiscuity, he didn't altogether reject the bohemian way of life he had come to love. For Lonnie, there was much about being a hippie, in seed form, that was compatible, and perhaps necessary, when it came to following Christ; in some ways the hippie's radical way of life was more akin to the authentic Christian life. In essence, Lonnie was the hippie with God's Spirit living inside him, what the hippie was meant to be.

No one saw this coming. Hippies were the last people Christians thought would turn to conventional religion. But that wasn't really the case with Lonnie. His passion was to recapture the radical, original call of the Christian, who walked by and in the Spirit for the sake of the lost—in power and demonstration, in fearlessness, in sold-out love. He helped revitalize and contemporize much of the American church but without renouncing Christianity's fundamental beliefs. It was a stripping away of dead religious tradition in favor of a spontaneous, living faith in Christ that was still biblically grounded. This was the heart behind the Jesus movement of the sixties and seventies, the Christian revolution in a time of revolutions.

In Riverside, Ruth and I would play a small but significant role in all of this, by God's grace, but before I begin telling that story, let me back up some years to when I first encountered these long-haired, bead-wearing, peace-toting hippies (including my deep-seated aversion for them) and how God gradually changed my heart and brought us together.

Before my garden experience, Ruth and I would go to Hollywood every so often. A lot of the male actors we saw at that time were beginning to wear their hair longer and wear looser fitting, flowy clothing. Well, I didn't like that; I thought they were being too effeminate. I made fun of them behind their backs, which Ruth got on my case about. Even though these weren't hippies, per se, they were the first signs I saw of the coming hippie movement.

You'd think that after becoming a born-again Christian, it would have been out of character for me to judge anyone. Unfortunately, that wasn't the case. As hippies gained more prominence and influence in our culture, the more my prejudice against them grew. I thought they were ruining our country, our youth. I saw them as enemies of the gospel, with their effeminate manners, loose morals, and irreverent attitude. The thought of a "real" Christian hippie never even crossed my mind; to me it was as oxymoronic as a Christian atheist.

I remember a hippie crossing in front of my car one day while I was waiting at a red light, and to my dismay he was carrying a Bible! *How dare he! He should be ashamed of himself!* I thought the so-called

Christian hippies, which were pretty rare, were worse than the secular ones because they were giving Christians a bad name. For all I know, though, this could've been Lonnie who had walked in front of my car.

In 1969 I had another run-in with some hippies. I was traveling with Dr. Frost around the state to different speaking engagements he was giving about the Holy Spirit. On one such occasion, we were scheduled for a meeting in Goleta, up near Santa Barbara. I had just bought a brand-new Cadillac, so we took my car. I had the sign of the fish decal on the back window, which by that time was a pretty popular thing to do. As we were just leaving Riverside, an old rattletrap pulled up alongside us on the freeway, full of these long-haired, dirty-looking hippie kids. I could see in my peripheral vision that some of them were trying to get my attention. My blood pressure immediately spiked. I hate to admit it now, but my initial reaction was to thumb my nose at them, which back then was like giving someone the finger. Anyway, just as I was about to do that, the Holy Spirit said, "What if they noticed the fish on the back of your car and knew what that meant?"

Boy, that stopped me cold. That thought no more than flashed through my mind, when I looked over and noticed that one of the kids in the backseat had bent down to pick up his Bible to show me; and whereas I had initially wanted to give him an insulting hand gesture, this kid was giving me the "one way" Jesus sign with his other hand, which was also hugely popular at the time.

Talk about being humbled quickly! I felt so convicted. To this day I wonder what might have happened to this kid had I followed through with my anger. I am so grateful God stopped me from potentially damaging that kid's faith with my judgementalism.

I was pretty torn up inside after that. Of course, Bob had no idea what was going on. I didn't breathe a word of it to him, because of my shame. It was obvious to me more than ever that God had a lot of work to do in my heart. All I could think to do in that moment was ask for forgiveness.

That was sometime in November. Now jump ahead to January. Ruth and I were in Palm Springs for a Christian Business Men Committee's (CBMC) regional convention over the weekend. (CBMC meetings were very similar to FGBM chapter meetings.) Sam Dalton was the first main speaker. Sam was pretty active among the CBMC chapters, particularly in Orange County, so I was pretty familiar with him. I always looked forward to his messages.

But his message that Friday morning wasn't his usual, "It's not skin but sin that separates us," that, as a black man, he liked to preach. Instead, Sam talked about how our holier-than-thou attitude toward hippies was doing terrible damage to the kingdom of God. He said, "A lot of parents and adults are sending their kids to hell, because they can't see past the long hair!" That was definitely hard to swallow. Then he said, "If you're guilty of that—if that's your problem—I want you to stand on your feet so I can pray for you."

I only had to think back a couple of months to know that I was guilty of what Sam was talking about. The shame and guilt were still pretty raw in my heart, and my aversion toward hippies was still unresolved. I needed healing.

There were somewhere around two thousand people at the convention that day, and I was one of only three people who stood up to be prayed for. It was very humbling. But like the scripture says, "Now is the day of salvation."[7] When you get the opportunity to be healed by God, you take it—no matter what the cost, no matter how alone it makes you feel. *At least I'm not completely alone,* I thought standing there.

After Sam prayed and I sat down, it was hard to tell if I felt any different about hippies when I brought them to mind. There were no hippies around, so I would have to wait to find out.

The meeting ended just in time for lunch. Our hotel was only a couple of blocks away from the convention in downtown Palm

Springs. Having walked to the convention, Ruth and I decided we'd stop for lunch on our way back to the hotel. At the first traffic signal we needed to cross, would you believe it, there were three hippie kids waiting to cross on the opposite side of the street as us—two guys and a young girl with a baby in her arms.

To my surprise, I noticed something different about myself right away: My blood pressure hadn't gone up. I wasn't feeling anything negative toward them. In fact, I felt love for them. Genuine love! The love of Christ! I wanted to talk to them.

The next part is a bit of a blur. I don't remember exactly how I approached them or how I worded it, but I ended up sharing the gospel with them there on the street! Perhaps even more miraculous than that, I was sharing so naturally, from the heart. It was the Spirit working through me. When I finished, one of the young men said, "Since this convention's been in town, we haven't been able to walk these streets without getting buttonholed by people trying to convert us. But I want you to know that you're the first person who's made any sense to me."

His remark caught me a bit by surprise; I think my brain had finally caught up with me. *Did I really just share the gospel with a bunch of strangers? Hippie strangers at that! Who was I?* It was all God. Only God could have healed me of my prejudice against hippies; only God could have used a "square" like me, more than twice the age of these kids, to effectively convey the gospel to them. That's the loving power, wisdom, and, should I say, humor of God at work.

Little did I know that God would soon have the most famous hippie of our time make an entry into our lives and our hearts for eternity—a divine encounter that led to many precious moments and adventures the Lord Jesus gave us together!

Twelve

Angels in Denmark

Fred:

A FEW WEEKS after our convention in Palm Springs in early 1970, a friend of mine by the name of Ray Brigham invited me to go with him on a mission trip to Denmark. Ray was originally from the Church of God out of Anderson, Indiana—a denomination that formed out of the Holiness movement. But when Ray got baptized in the Holy Spirit, he quickly became *persona non grata.*

Ray and his wife then moved out to California and started a ministry called Inter-Church Renewal Ministries. (In fact, it was through Ray's ministry that we got involved with Dr. Frost.) As the name suggests, Ray's ministry was aimed at unifying Christians from all denominations under the teaching that included the experience of the baptism of the Holy Spirit, which they did primarily through sharing testimonies at luncheon meetings. Ray himself was passionate about seeing Catholics baptized in the Holy Spirit. His deepest desire was to one day share the reality of the baptism of the Holy Spirit with the pope.

Let me give a little background as to how this mission trip came about. At one of his luncheons, Ray met a landscape contractor. I don't remember his name, so let's call him Jim. This man Jim was once a Campus Crusade leader. As with Ray, when the Campus Crusade leadership found out Jim had received the baptism of the Holy Spirit and was openly speaking in tongues, they disassociated themselves with him, to put it nicely. This didn't stop Jim from doing what he loved doing most: evangelizing. Only now, instead of going to colleges and universities, Jim took his outreach experience and his newfound empowerment through the Holy Spirit to outdoor malls, which had become hubs for a lot of teenage misfits and delinquents. Jim led dozens of these kids to the Lord, many of whom were druggies and drop-outs; he also led them into the baptism of the Holy Spirit. Naturally, my friend Ray was interested in Jim's work.

"Could you bring some of these kids to the next luncheon?" Ray asked.

"Sure. They'd be happy to come and share."

At the following meeting, Jim brought twenty or so of these former misfits turned Jesus freaks. I was there. They shared their testimonies, and it was quite powerful and moving to hear. I saw with my own eyes their transformations in Christ. It was also incredibly encouraging to know that kids like these, whom many of us deemed too far gone to be reached, actually *could* be reached. They weren't hippies, but just as countercultural. Now they were countercultural in another way—*for the kingdom!*

Soon after, Ray took a bucket-list trip to Rome that his daughter, who worked for Scandinavian Airlines, set up for him as a gift. (It was looking like Ray might get his chance to speak to the pope after all.) Before Rome, Ray spent a few days in Copenhagen. A friend of Ray's, a Spirit-filled Reformed pastor from Minneapolis, happened to be staying at the same hotel. When they ran into each other, Ray's friend told him that he'd heard about this town not far outside of Copenhagen where the Spirit of God was allegedly moving very powerfully, particularly in this one church.

"I'm heading out there to check it out. You should come!"

Ray agreed to go.

However, when they arrived, it wasn't quite the move of God they were expecting. A big controversy was raging, and not just in the town, but all over Denmark: The second annual international sex fair was to take place in a few months' time in Odense, and the conservatives and religious of the country were not happy about it. I mentioned earlier that the sixties were a kind of cultural crucible in America, but America wasn't alone. Denmark was considered the epicenter of the sexual revolution that swept through the West in the 1960s. It had, by far, the most liberal laws in the world when it came to pornography, prostitution, and drugs. People from all over the world, mostly young men, were flocking there to have a "good time." To this day Denmark is one of the most liberal countries in the world.

It was in this cultural climate that Denmark hosted its first international sex fair—a huge financial success and tourism boost for the country. From a financial point of view, then, it only made sense to make it an annual event. Many were morally outraged, and pastors and clergymen from all over the country and from various Christian denominations had written to the government, pleading with them to cancel the event. But the government wasn't budging.

This was the controversy that Ray and his friend walked into when they arrived in this little Danish town. Churches were gathering regularly to discuss what could be done and to pray. Ray and his friend listened in on one such gathering, and it was during the middle of this meeting, while everyone was praying, that a woman there had a vision. In her vision she saw numerous angels descending on Copenhagen. She told this to everyone and added that she believed it had something to do with the sex fair. How, she didn't know. That's when it hit Ray: He knew how. He said, "I think I have the interpretation to your vision. I want to bring a team back from America to evangelize to the people at the sex fair. I have the perfect people for that." He had in mind, of course, the kids Jim brought to his luncheon.

The group thought this was a good idea and told Ray to keep in touch so that they could work out the details.

A couple of days later Ray left for Rome. Unfortunately, Ray never got his chance to speak with the pope, but with the way things had unexpectedly turned out in Denmark, Ray had plenty to think about and do. Back in the States, Ray told Jim everything that had happened in Denmark and asked him if it was possible to fly some of his kids out there. Jim was on board for it all. They decided they would take seventy-five kids.

Everything was being made ready to go. A date was set, and with the help of his daughter, Ray chartered a half-passenger, half-cargo plane to get them all there. Then some complications arose about the in-country living arrangements. Originally, all the kids were arranged to stay in the homes of parishioners, but this was suddenly no longer a possibility. Ray had to fly out to Denmark and meet with the church leaders of that town to smooth things over; otherwise, the trip would be cancelled. It took a while, but in the end Ray was able to convince them to allow his kids to sleep in the basements of their churches. Better than nothing, I guess.

During the middle of all this, a drunken sailor barged into the church where they were meeting. He immediately started harassing one of the pastors. Apparently, this sailor had gotten a young woman from that church pregnant some time back. Having conceived out of wedlock, she went to her pastor for advice, and he advised her to have nothing to do with this guy anymore. And that's what she did.

Well, the sailor didn't appreciate this pastor interfering in his life like that. From then on, whenever he found himself back in town after being out at sea, he made it a point to pay this pastor a visit and give him hell—that is, after he got nice and drunk.

Just about everyone there that day was familiar with this man and his drunken antics. While this confrontation was taking place, the secretary of the church turned to Ray and said irritably to him, "If you're such a man of God, save this drunken sailor." (Many who were there listening to Ray plead his case on behalf of these kids had begun questioning Ray's authenticity as a Christian; this was part of the problem that needed smoothing over.)

In his defense, Ray responded, "I'm not God. You can't do that to me. It's not up to me," which promptly quieted her.

Anyway, the episode with the drunken man was taken care of quickly, and the meeting resumed. The mission trip was back on.

Meanwhile, Ruth and I were in the middle of a church program at All Saints called Experiment of Faith that Father Bellis started after he had read Samuel Shoemaker's book by the same name. Samuel Shoemaker was one of the founders of Alcoholics Anonymous. In his book, Shoemaker describes his time in China as a missionary. Watching how the Pentecostal missionaries evangelized the Chinese revolutionized Shoemaker's approach to evangelism. He saw that they were leading people *to Christ*, not to some specific denomination. Having grown up in the Episcopal Church, where most church members were born into the faith, this was mind-blowing for him.

The program at All Saints was an implementation of Shoemaker's core tenets found in the book. Twenty of us signed up for the six weeks it would take; I was one of the leaders. When Ray asked me if I wanted to go to Denmark with him and I agreed, I hadn't realized that we would be flying out before the sixth and final session took place, which would be culminating in an evangelism "simulation" that we came up with to apply what we'd learned from the previous five weeks.

I had no choice but to tell Father Bellis the unfortunate news that I would be out of town on that date, but I didn't tell him why I was going to be out of town. I was a bit nervous about explaining to my priest that the reason one of his leaders couldn't make it was because I was taking a large group of teenagers to evangelize outside of an international sex fair. No matter how I worded it in my head, I couldn't imagine him approving of such a thing or understanding the prospect. Fortunately, he didn't ask too many questions.

But then on the night I was to leave, Father Bellis called me up to wish me well on my trip and asked, "By the way, where'd you say you were going?"

"Well, I didn't exactly say," I said. "I wasn't sure you would approve."

To my surprise, when I explained the trip to him, he said, "Fred, that sounds amazing! When you get back I want to meet with you. This could be something you could share with the whole congregation."

"Sure thing," I said.

Phew.

My team and I left for Denmark that night. In addition to the seventy-five teenage kids, there were three chaperones: Ray, Dr. Frost, and myself. This also happened to be when I first made acquaintance with the young Lonnie Frisbee. A woman from Calvary Chapel in Costa Mesa had heard about the trip, and when she found out that a ticket on Ray's chartered plane was only seventy-five dollars, she bought two for Kenn Gulliksen (a good friend of Lonnie's and the original founder of the Vineyard church) and his wife, Joanie, as a honeymoon gift. But then Joanie said to Kenn, "I don't think I should go; I think God wants you to give my ticket to Lonnie instead." So that's how Lonnie came to be on the trip, and even though we wouldn't get to know one another personally during this time, it inaugurated what would become a lasting and impactful relationship.

One of the first things I noticed when we got to Copenhagen was just how pervasive sex was. Pornography was not only normal for the Danes, it was celebrated. It was everywhere, just out in the open. When we visited Walking Street (a very long and famous pedestrian-only shopping area, kind of like our Rodeo Drive in Beverly Hills but without the cars), as charming and full of history as it was, it was just about ruined with all the lewd and pornographic advertising we saw in plain sight. There was no way of not seeing it, unless you stared at the ground or sky the whole time.

Our experience in Copenhagen really set the tone for the whole trip. We got a good idea of the spiritual and moral climate we would be up against during our time at the sex fair in Odense. We knew we would need the Holy Spirit.

Just to be clear, we didn't go into the sex fair itself, which was held inside a large convention center. The plan was to street-evangelize and minister to those outside the fair, either going in or out. Our prayer was twofold: salvations first and foremost, but if nothing else, keeping people out of the sex fair.

Our first day in Odense, the kids took to the streets fearlessly for Christ. Dr. Frost and I were so impressed. Impressed not only with their boldness, but also with their instant success. Dr. Frost and I looked at each other at one point and said, "Man, what're we gonna do?" We felt so lame standing on the sidelines, but we couldn't do *that!* I mean, that kind of stop-them-in-their-tracks witnessing was totally foreign to us.

It wasn't like these kids were specially trained evangelists. They were just being obedient, and their strategy was pretty straightforward, using Billy Graham's famous "Four Steps To Having Peace With God" gospel tract: Step 1: "God loves you and wants you to experience peace—life-abundant and eternal." Step 2: "But sin separates us from God." Step 3: "The Cross is our only remedy." Step 4: "Receive the gift of Christ as Lord and Savior." It ends with the Sinner's Prayer.

The more I watched them, the more I thought, *I could do that.* Then I remembered the encounter I had with the hippies in downtown Palm Springs, how sharing the gospel with them came so naturally because of my newfound genuine love I felt for them. They were strangers to me just as much as the people walking the streets of Odense were to me now.

"We have to do this! We have to be a part of this!" I finally told Dr. Frost. We took a step of faith and went out there—and it was amazing!

When it came down to it, we just wanted people to know there was a greater love out there—an inexhaustible, divine love, a love far more powerful and gratifying than anything they were seeking and hoping to come away with at the sex fair. That was what compelled us. I had to look at them with the eyes of Christ—with Love. It was as simple as that, really.

As the week went by, I found it a little hard to believe just how well the gospel was being received, given where we were. It helped, I'm sure, that we could break the ice a bit with the fact that we were Americans. When someone finds out you've traveled across the world just to talk with them, a stranger, I suppose that person is more inclined to listen. To be honest, I was expecting more spiritual warfare, but it was as if the angels were shielding us from attacks of the enemy. Each night after hours of witnessing, we convened as a group and debriefed. We heard about miracles on top of salvations. A little girl was healed of deafness, for example. All in all, about fifteen hundred people came to the Lord over the course of the ten days we were in Denmark. In fact, I'm a firm believer that this outreach helped launch a revival in all of Scandinavia.

But perhaps the most amazing thing that happened on the trip (for me, anyway) didn't take place until the day of our flight back to the States.

It was early morning on Easter Sunday. Dr. Frost and I were in our room about to head down for breakfast, when we got a knock on the door. It was Ray.

"I've got a guy out here I really want you two to meet and pray for before we leave Denmark," he said.

"All right," I said. "Bring him in."

A young man walked in, who looked somewhere in his late twenties. He told us just two things about himself: He was from Finland and he was a die-hard atheist. *Looks like we've got our work cut out for us,* I thought. When we started sharing the gospel with him, he showed as much interest in what we were saying as a blind person shows interest in light. *Why did Rob want us to share with this guy, anyway?* But we kept trucking along. We shared for about an hour, just the two of us blabbing away at someone who might as well have not been there at all. I mean, the guy's face was as blank as could be. At one point we tried using the gospel tract that had been so successful on the street, but we couldn't even get the guy past step one. He didn't care that God loved him, because, well, he didn't believe in God. How do you convince someone to at least believe that there is more to this life than what meets the eye?

By the end of the hour Dr. Frost and I had just about run out of strategies. Then Bob came up with an idea: "Why don't you share your story at the Garden Tomb?" he suggested.

It couldn't hurt, I thought. The whole time we had been sharing the gospel in a broad, universal way. Maybe a more personal approach would work.

For the better part of my story the guy looked as lifeless and bored as before. But when I got to the part of my story when I prayed the simple prayer, "God, if you're really real, reveal yourself to me," something began to change in him. When I was done with my story and said to him, "Now, if there's any part of you that wants to know whether God is real, I want you to pray that prayer with me," God finally broke through this young man's stony exterior. To our utter disbelief, he went ahead with the prayer just as I had suggested: "God, if you're really real, reveal yourself to me."

Like a time-lapse of a flower blooming from a bud, his whole countenance brightened. Suddenly he was on his knees, without us even telling him to do so, asking Jesus to come into his life, for God to be real in his life, for God to forgive him. It was an absolutely beautiful, miraculous divine encounter.

And then just as quickly as he had said that prayer, he said he had to go and left. *What just happened?* we thought.

Later during breakfast, we told Ray about it.

"Do you know who that guy was?" Ray asked with a huge smile on his face.

"No," we answered.

"That was that drunken sailor who stormed into church that one day, the same guy the angry secretary told me to save."

"That guy?" I asked in disbelief.

"That's the guy!"

I was speechless. We had thought this guy was just some stranger Ray had met that morning but didn't have time to share the gospel with. What a miracle it was, I then thought, that this conversion happened just as we were about to leave, at the eleventh hour, so to speak, as if by pure design and providence. Now knowing who the man was, I could see that it *was* by design and providence! Like Joseph said to his brothers in Genesis, "You intended to harm me, but God intended it for good to accomplish what is now being done, the saving of many lives."[8]

At the airport, just as we were about to board our plane, a woman approached us—the woman who had had the vision of angels. News of the drunken sailor's salvation had traveled fast, apparently. She was carrying with her a handful of porcelain Danish angels, which she gave to each one of the adults as we boarded the plane. It was her way of saying thank you and that we were the angels in her vision—and I guess we really were, although I certainly didn't feel like an angel. I'll say it again, and I'll say it as many times as I have to: It was 100 percent all God!

Thirteen
Planting and Sowing

Fred:

WHEN WE RETURNED to Riverside, my pastor asked me to share the story of our trip with the congregation, but I reminded Father Bellis, "You know, the things we were doing over there were not very Episcopalian. I think we ought to have lunch first so I can share with you what happened." He thought that was a good idea.

So we met, and I told him everything that happened on our trip from beginning to end.

"Fred, you need to share this with the church," Father Bellis said. "You're a layman, and Copenhagen is a long ways away—it needs to be you who shares. I'm in no position to share for you."

I said, "Okay, I'll do it."

The following Sunday I spoke in all three services. After the second service, which was always the most well attended, Father Bellis told the congregation, "If anyone's interested in knowing more about the kind of evangelizing Fred did in Denmark, please stay behind before going to coffee hour."

About a dozen people stayed behind. I took them through the four steps to peace with God. Most were middle-aged, but there were a couple of younger people too. One was a teenager named John, whom I was very surprised to see.

John's mother was one of the twenty parishioners who went through the Experiment in Faith program. I got to know her and learned she was a respected teacher and the dean of women at a local high school; her husband, John's stepdad, was a representative for the California Teachers Association. One day she confided with me about her son, whom she was *very* worried about. John had started hanging out with the wrong crowd and was getting into some trouble, so she asked if I could pray for him. Not long after this, I received a call from her: John had been arrested for peddling drugs; he was only fifteen. She was pleading for my help. I said I definitely would in any way I could.

When John was let out of jail a few days later, his mom and stepdad brought him over for dinner. They were hoping Ruth and I could leave a positive influence on him, perhaps get him interested in church or maybe even get him saved! At first, it seemed promising. When John stepped into our home at the Ranch, he looked around and said, "Well, if *this* is the establishment, it doesn't look too bad." You see, there was a popular saying going around: "Resist authority!" It was 1969, and there was a deep distrust in government and religion among the youth. I guess John didn't feel too threatened by us initially, for whatever reason.

But despite our best efforts, we couldn't get through to him. He was pretty closed-off for most of the dinner, which made for a bit of an awkward night. I felt bad for John's mother especially; she was really hoping something would "click" in her son that night.

Going back to that Sunday when I shared: This was why I was surprised to see John in that group. If that dinner was any indication of John's spiritual condition, my guess would have been that Christian evangelism would have been near the bottom of his list of interests. But here he was! Even more surprising, John approached me after and said, "I just want to tell you that I enjoyed your talk." *Where was all this coming from?* I thought. *Where was* this *kid during the dinner?*

Sensing this was a divine encounter of sorts, I asked John the question you find at the end of Billy Graham's tract, the same question we had just gone over: "John, wouldn't you like to make that commitment to Christ and experience the things I was talking about today?"

He thought for a second and then said, "Yes, I would." *Hallelujah! Wait till his mother hears about this!* So I prayed with John right there to receive Christ as his Lord and Savior. What a miraculous turn of events.

The next day I wanted to give something to John to commemorate his new spiritual birthday that could benefit his growth in Christ in the days and months (hopefully years) to come. I had the perfect gift in mind. After I came to Christ in the garden, Ruth bought me a brand-new leather-bound Oxford New Testament. They used goatskin leather and India paper—it was a work of art! I cherished it; I still have it to this day. Plus, it was small enough to carry around. I went down to the Bible bookstore and bought one, put John's name on it in gold lettering, wrote the date of his conversion on the inside—you know, the works. I wanted it to be something really special, something he kept and used for a long time.

About a week after I had given my gift to John, I got a distressed call from his mother, saying, "Oh, Fred. John's in trouble again."

"What's going on?" I asked.

"He stole a motorcycle."

"He stole a motorcycle?!"

"Yes. He did it to go see his biological father in San Diego, and now he's in juvenile hall. I don't know what to do. Will you please help me? Can you go see him and talk to him? I think he'll listen to you. He doesn't want anything to do with me."

What can I do? I thought. Not that I didn't want to help, but I was almost fifty years old and he was fifteen. Why would he listen to *me?* His mother sounded desperate, though, and was counting on me, so I said, "I'll see what I can do."

Inside the jail's visitor's center, they had these little cubicles that were about six-feet high so that you could talk with some privacy, just like you see in the movies. I didn't have to wait long for John to show up. From the second he sat down across from me, it was clear as day he didn't want to talk. I couldn't get him to even look me in the eye. The whole time I was there John was staring at the ceiling, slouched in his chair, tapping his foot impatiently.

The old John was back, the one who wanted to shut the whole world out. *What happened? Where was the John from last week, the one who prayed with me?* I mean, I couldn't imagine jail being any fun, but I thought John would be a little happy to see me. I told him I wasn't there to lecture him, that I wasn't disappointed either. "We all make mistakes. I just want to help and to encourage you to trust in Jesus. God still loves you—more than you can ever know. One little slip-up is not going to change that fact."

But it was the dinner all over again. All my advice and encouragement fell on deaf ears. I remember thinking, *Man, I'm really making points here. He probably hates my guts; to him I'm just his mom's messenger.* I dreaded the conversation I would be having with her very soon.

When time was up, John stood up to leave, and as he turned around, I noticed something in his back pocket: the New Testament I gave him! It was folded in half and in pretty bad shape from the looks of it, probably from being sat on. In any other context, my immediate reaction would have been to take offense: *He should know better than to treat the Bible that way!* But instead, I thought, *He still has his Bible! There's hope!* Something was compelling him to keep it; maybe he was even reading it. Seeing that Bible was the silver lining in what had previously been an all but pointless trip.

I called John's mother to tell her how it went: "He really didn't want anything to do with me," I said. "But I saw he still has his Bible with him of his own free accord, and that's something to be encouraged about."

"What do I do when he gets out?" she asked.

"John needs to be surrounded by strong Christians his age," I advised. "What John *really* needs is to be filled with the Holy Spirit, because that's the difference maker. By themselves, Christians don't have the strength to change, but with the Holy Spirit, they have that power."

"How do we do all that?" she asked.

"Let's take it one step at a time," I said. "Let me take him up to the San Fernando Valley to meet the kids I traveled to Denmark with. If John wants, they can pray for him and share their stories. I think John will really like them."

I felt good about this plan. Then some of our friends from Orange, who were part of our Bible study down there, reminded me that Lonnie Frisbee was speaking every Wednesday night at Calvary Chapel in Costa Mesa.

"The kids are just flocking in," they said. "He packs out the place."

I had heard how powerful and anointed Lonnie was as a speaker. Salvations were coming in by the droves in that little church that Chuck Smith founded and pastored.

That's exactly what John needs right now, I thought excitedly.

I made arrangements with John's mom to pick him up on a Wednesday afternoon once he was out of juvie. Calvary Chapel at that time was meeting inside a little chapel, so seating was pretty limited. As I'd come to find out, if you didn't get to one of Lonnie's meetings early enough, there was a good chance you would have to stand outside. There was always a small overflow crowd of people looking in through the chapel's large front windows; outside speakers were also rigged for sound.

I picked John up around four o' clock in the afternoon, wanting to make sure we got seats to give him the best possible chance of encountering God.

This was in the middle of August, and Riverside in August is *hot*. Even so, John walked out his front door wearing a heavy army jacket and hood over his head. The whole way to the car he had his head down and sulked. Clearly he was unhappy and probably being forced to go against his will. Since this was all my idea, I felt bad. I even tried brightening his mood by getting him a cheeseburger through a drive-thru and letting him eat in the car—something I never let my own children do—but I couldn't even get a thank you from him.

Hopefully Lonnie has more success than me, I thought.

We made it to the chapel with plenty of time to spare. As expected, the place was packed out. When the worship got going, I remember all the teenagers singing a Children of the Day song that went "*Love, love, love, love.*" Some had their arms around each other, swaying to the music. Others had their hands stretched out up in the air in praise. Kids were clapping and dancing. There was hardly a face in that chapel that wasn't beaming with joy. The Spirit of God was definitely there.

There was one face, however, that wasn't filled with joy: John's. For the better part of worship his hood was still on, his arms were folded, and he was as stiff as a statue. As the worship continued, however, his demeanor relaxed a bit, and by the end his hood had come off and he even started clapping a little bit. *Improvement! It's working,* I thought.

As soon as the music ended and we all sat down to hear Lonnie, the hood went back on and the arms refolded. He was flatlining again; I was losing him. My hope was that Lonnie, in all of his anointing and charisma, would bring John back to life and that John would go up and recommit his life to the Lord for the altar call. But none of that happened.

When Lonnie finished, Chuck Smith announced that they were going to be having a baptismal service next Saturday at Corona del Mar. I wondered if John would be interested in going to that, so as we were leaving I asked him. I couldn't even get a headshake out of him. Just silence.

I went home that night feeling a bit like a failure. This kid was an enigma.

A day or so later I got a call from John's mom. "Fred, what's this about John being baptized this Saturday?" she asked.

I tried acting like I wasn't surprised by her question, but in all reality I was shocked. I could've sworn John wanted nothing to do with that. The Holy Spirit was clearly working on John in ways that I couldn't see. So I told her about the baptismal.

"Well," she said, "we can't let John get baptized all by himself. His family needs to be there. Could we go too?" (In the Anglican Church, when you're baptized, it's tradition to have your whole family there, including godparents, and afterwards there's a big party. Baptism is a big deal.)

I said, "Sure! That would be wonderful."

We took a whole caravan of people to the beach the following Saturday. (In addition to John and his family, the group that I walked through Billy Graham's tract went too.) There was already a huge crowd when we got there at Pirate's Cove in Corona del Mar. Anyone familiar with Lonnie probably recognizes him from pictures taken at these mass baptisms. He and several other leaders from Calvary Chapel baptized hundreds at Pirate's Cove over one summer.

Pirate's Cove, Newport Beach

Lonnie was easily recognizable back then, resembling what many people imagine Jesus looking like: long hair, long beard, skinny, with simple, natural-looking clothing on. Watching him baptize people—bare-chested, ascetic-looking, bright smile—was like looking at someone who had been pulled straight from the pages of the Bible and inserted into the twentieth century.

At Pirate's Cove, people were fanned all over the big rocks and cliffs that overlooked the beach; hundreds more were down below, some waiting to be baptized, others worshipping God. A small band was playing worship songs down by the water, using the horseshoe-shaped cove as natural amplification. Their songs made their way through the crowds like slow-moving electricity. Everyone was singing. It was a heavenly scene.

The song I remember the most from that day went like this: "*Jesus said, 'Come to the water, stand by my side. I know you are thirsty; you won't be denied. I felt every teardrop when in darkness you cried; and I strove to remind you that for those tears I died.*'"[9]

We found a place to sit on the rocks, up high. We could see Lonnie in the distance, waist-deep in the water, praying for people, dunking them. Kenn Gulliksen and Tom Stipes were out there too, baptizing. Then we made our way down to the water so that John could be baptized. When Lonnie baptized John, it looked like Jesus baptizing him. Well, it *was* Jesus—through Lonnie. We all gave John the biggest hugs as he walked from the shore, then we just worshipped and basked in the moment until it was all over and time to go home.

When we got back to the Ranch, John was a changed person. His whole aura had transformed: no more slouched shoulders, no more averting eye contact, no more hoodie hiding his face. It was like he had stepped into the light. He was friendly and responsive. There was a new warmth to him, a new heartbeat.

We all gathered in my living room for the afterparty. At one point Ruth walked over to John and, seeing that he had his New Testament with him, asked, "Why don't you open up your Bible and see what God has to say to you on your baptismal day?"

"Okay," John replied. He opened it to a random page and read the first verse he saw: "Therefore we were buried with him through baptism into death, that just as Christ was raised from the dead by the glory of the Father, even so we also should walk in newness of life"—Romans 6:4.

John's stepdad, who was sitting next to me on the living room steps, exclaimed, "John! How did you . . . how'd you find that?"

"I just opened it up," John replied.

Ruth and I sensed this was a divine encounter—and so did John's stepdad, who committed his life to Christ a week later.

I guess sometimes a person's salvation, or path to salvation, doesn't happen all at once, but rather in stages. A pitstop here, a bump in the road there. For John, it was like the Holy Spirit had brought him to Christ little by little, like removing layers in order to get to the heart: God was in control, not me. That was the lesson I learned, anyhow. Which goes to show that you never know what God is secretly doing inside someone's heart. Of course, I had my role: I did some of the "planting" and "sowing." But ultimately it was God who brought growth and faith in John. It was God who brought John to himself and saved him. Praise the Lord!

Fourteen
Sunday at All Saints

Ruth:

AFTER JOHN'S baptism, Fred and I started taking groups to Calvary Chapel Costa Mesa every Wednesday night to hear Lonnie speak. We'd also go on Friday nights to listen to Kenn Gulliksen. We did this for about a month. During this time, the Holy Spirit spoke to Fred while he was driving on the freeway: "What Lonnie is doing at Calvary Chapel shouldn't be happening there *only,* it should be happening all over."

Fred thought, "You're right, Lord, but how do we do that?"

"Bring Lonnie to Riverside. Invite him to speak at All Saints."

So Fred went to Father Bellis to tell him what he felt God was saying.

"Maybe Lonnie can do what he does in Costa Mesa," Fred said, "but at All Saints too—a weekly evening service."

Father Bellis liked the idea. "I'm not sure what the vestry will think, though," he said. "I'll have to get their permission first before I give you the green light."

Meanwhile, Fred and I prayed about it more. We thought if the word Fred received truly was from God, then God would find a way to bring Lonnie up here.

A few days later Father Bellis reconnected with Fred. "The vestry has agreed to let Lonnie speak on Sunday nights. Also, I convinced them to give him a stipend to help with the cost. However, the vestry wanted me to make it crystal clear to you that this is *your thing*. You'll be running it and supervising it. In other words, if people start throwing rocks—heads up, because they'll be coming your way!"

That may sound harsh, but it's important to understand that having a charismatic service in an Episcopal church came with some big risks. When it came to a person like Lonnie, there was always the possibility of ruffling some feathers along the way. Father Bellis was no less than putting his neck on the line for Fred; several priests throughout the country had recently been asked to leave their churches because they had veered too far from traditional Anglicanism. Father Bellis was basically telling Fred, "Be careful." As a priest, he had his own flock to take care of.

"I completely understand," Fred told him.

Now that Fred had Father Bellis's blessing, he went to Lonnie and Chuck Smith about it.

"When do I start?" was pretty much Lonnie's response to Fred's proposition. He was not the kind of person to turn down a chance to proclaim Christ, especially from the pulpit.

Both Lonnie and Chuck thought it was a great idea, so with all of our ducks pretty much in order, the only things left to do were to pray and promote.

We enlarged a magazine photo of Lonnie, with his long hair and beard, preaching to a multitude of people on a California beach and made lots of flyers and a few posters. We advertised the Sunday evening meeting at All Saints and invited everyone to come and hear Lonnie Frisbee, the hippie evangelist!

Downtown Riverside at that time had been turned into an outdoor mall that was supposed to revitalize the downtown area but was mostly a failure because the city couldn't get new businesses to come or stay. Instead of it becoming a family-friendly shopping area, downtown Riverside became a popular hangout spot for troubled kids and drug dealers. In other words, it was the perfect place to tell some kids about Jesus and invite them to church.

Being fresh off his trip to Denmark, Fred said to us, "Every Friday night we'll take a group of kids down to the mall and witness and pass out the flyers. We'll go two by two like we did in Denmark."

"Oh, honey," I said, "I don't think I can do that. I'm nervous about those kids over there."

But when you're married to a hardheaded Norwegian, he usually ends up getting his way: "Jesus said, 'I am with you always.' You have nothing to fear."

He was right, although that didn't really make the fear go away for me.

As planned, we split up in groups of twos when we arrived there on Friday evening. I partnered with a woman close to my age. We were given a stack of flyers and a couple of Billy Graham's Four Steps tracts and then ventured out.

"All right," I said nervously. "Since we're here, let's hurry up and get this over with, and then we can go home." Before we approached anyone, though, we agreed that one of us would do the talking while the other did the praying. I said I would do the talking.

It didn't take us long into the evening to home in on two young girls sitting down on a grassy lawn.

"Come on," I said. "Let's talk to them."

We walked up to them, and I said, "We have something we'd like to share with you. Do you have time?"

"Yeah, we have time," they said.

So we sat down with them, and I began to share the Four Steps—all the while my partner was faithfully praying. The Four Steps tract is nice because it does most of the work explaining the gospel for you in an understandable way, but I was getting nervous about the *big question* at the end. *What if they say no? I'm not sure I'll be able to handle it.* Then the moment of truth came. I asked the question: "Is there any reason why you wouldn't like to accept Jesus in your life right now?"

"I would," one of the girls said.

"You *would?*" I said, totally shocked and elated. "That's wonderful! And what about you, honey?" I then asked the other girl. "Would you like to accept Jesus into your heart today?"

"Yes," she said with a smile.

Wow! I thought. *God is so good! Why was I so afraid?*

The next thing I knew, we were praying with these girls to receive Jesus into their hearts. It was amazing! It was the best feeling in the world.

Then I noticed these two guys walking our way.

"Here come our boyfriends," the girls said.

Oh dear, I thought, the fear returning. *What are they going to say when they find out their girlfriends accepted Jesus?*

I looked around; Fred was nowhere in sight. Under my breath I said a quick prayer, "Jesus, you've got to help us!"

I could tell these boys were high on something as they got closer. I said to my partner in a low voice, "We can't be afraid. We have to share with them. Just keep praying."

After we stood up to greet them and I looked into this one boy's eyes, God took all the fear away—it was so beautiful. I shared with them what I had shared with the girls. One of the boys told me he was the son of a Baptist minister but had walked away from his parents' faith. I encouraged him not to give up his search for God, that God was much bigger than any denomination, and that, most importantly, it's a relationship with Christ that God wants from us. I don't think the boys sat down the entire time I was talking; and although they didn't accept Christ like their girlfriends had, we were able to plant the seed of Jesus's love in them and hand them flyers to our Sunday night meeting.

From that point forward I was much less afraid to go out and witness. I realized, firsthand, that by myself I'm a pretty timid person, but with the Holy Spirit, I can be bold and effective for the Lord. He wins the battles for you! You just have to offer yourself to him—and then he'll do the rest!

That first Sunday night meeting with Lonnie we had seventy-five kids come. Not bad! Three committed their lives to Christ. In fact, one of them was the teenage daughter of the senior warden at All

Saints. The next day she went to Father Bellis and told him, "I was planning to go with some friends again up in the mountains to drop some acid, but I asked Jesus into my heart last night and I don't need drugs anymore!" What a testimony!

Pretty soon our church was packed every Sunday night. The kids absolutely loved it, just like they did at the Costa Mesa church. Now, seeing that we were a church plant inside another church, we had to be very respectful of our surroundings. In other words, we couldn't do anything *too crazy*, so we left the "crazy stuff" for our afterglow meetings that we had afterward at our Ranch, which we actually carried over from our Bible study days. Everyone was invited as long as we could accommodate them. A big caravan of cars filled our driveway each week. This was our way of providing a ministry time for these kids and a safe place for them to experience and exercise the gifts of the Spirit, especially for those who had just accepted Christ and wanted to receive the baptism of the Holy Spirit.

Fred and I had another really interesting incident at the mall. During one of our Friday night outings, we noticed a teenage boy all by himself playing his guitar. He looked pretty dejected, so we went over and shared the gospel with him. He didn't accept Christ, unfortunately, but we invited him to the Sunday night meeting anyway. He said he'd think about it. I felt really sorry for him; I just wanted to make him smile and feel less alone.

"Why don't you bring your guitar with you and play a song or two for everyone?" I offered. I'm not sure what I was thinking. I'm pretty sure he was high when we were talking to him, and chances were he'd come to church high too. In any case, he didn't show up that Sunday. As far as we knew, he never came.

About a year or so later, Fred decided he wanted to take some guitar lessons. He had learned a little bit by playing with kids from our meetings. Excited about this, he then bought a half dozen guitars to give away so that he could teach others what he had learned, which was when Fred realized he might have to learn more for himself. Soon after, Fred saw a sign in the window of a music store advertising guitar lessons and made an appointment.

The teacher was a young hippie-type.

"I'm not interested in a lot of the rock and roll music of today and that sort of thing," Fred told his teacher on his first lesson. "Really, all I want to be able to do is to play some of these Christian songs and choruses." This led to Fred telling his teacher about the work he was doing at All Saints.

"You know, that's really interesting," the young man said. "That's where I found Jesus."

"You did?" Fred asked, surprised.

"I was down at the mall in Riverside about a year ago—really out of it—when an old couple approached me out of the blue, shared Jesus with me, and invited me to come to their church. I didn't go right away, but a few a months later I went. I remember seeing from my car an elderly man hugging everyone who came in."

"That was me!" Fred said. "And that old couple was also me and my wife. I remember you now!"

In that first year alone, when Lonnie was teaching and preaching, a thousand young people committed their lives to the Lord. We know that number because we handed out a thousand New Testaments, which we gave to those who had accepted Christ during our meetings. We also gave away the Ichthys decal that Fred had developed and these little aluminum crosses that Father Bellis provided.

Sometime during our first year, a married couple came to one of our Sunday night meetings. The wife had been invited by one of the All Saints kids at the grocery store where she worked as a cashier. She said she would come and somehow convinced her religion-hating biker husband to go too. He was one of these guys who dressed in all black and wore a big mustache and a bandana around his head. Real mean-looking.

They sat up on the balcony of the church during the service. When Lonnie was done preaching and gave his usual altar call, this gal came running down from the balcony to receive Christ, weeping. About twenty feet behind her was her husband, coming after her, looking like the devil himself. It was clear to everyone he did not want his wife to have anything to do with Jesus. Before he was able to reach her, however, Fred stepped in front of him and said, "She's okay. She's okay. She just wants to commit her life to the Lord."

And then the strangest thing happened. It wouldn't have taken much to get Fred out of the way; the man was much bigger and stronger than Fred, not to mention he was enraged. But he just stood there, inexplicably, as if a wall had dropped down between them. He wasn't even acknowledging Fred; he just kept looking around him to see what was going on with his wife.

By now she was praying with Lonnie to receive Christ into her heart. I could see that Fred was saying something to her husband, who still couldn't get past Fred. Whatever he was saying wasn't calming the man down, in fact quite the opposite. Yet no matter how angry he became, he wasn't going anywhere.

Fred told me later that the Holy Spirit revealed to him that it was an evil spirit that was manifesting in this man and that Fred needed to pray in tongues in order to bind the demon. What no one knew at this time, except for the man who was himself manifesting, was that as Fred was praying, multiple demons were leaving the man's body—through his eyes! That's what the man later said: He could literally see demons exiting his body from out of his eyes. When we found this out, it made a lot of sense because, thinking back, the man's demeanor changed from angry and defiant to peaceful and submissive very quickly. It was night and day!

Suddenly free from his demonic oppression, he finally looked at Fred.

"What's your name?" Fred asked.

"Kurt."

"Kurt, would you pray the Sinner's Prayer with me and accept Christ into your life?"

"Yes."

It was one of the most dramatic conversions and divine encounters I had ever seen, not to mention that his wife had also accepted Christ in pretty dramatic fashion moments before. There was so much God-energy and love in that place immediately following . . . we were practically swimming in it.

But their story doesn't end there. As infants they had been baptized in the Lutheran Church, but now that they had personally committed their lives to Christ, they wanted to get baptized again and went to Father Bellis about this. Under normal circumstances Father Bellis would have denied them a second baptism because the Anglican Church considers infant baptism valid; a second baptism would be the same as saying infant baptisms are no good.

Prior to this couple's request, there had been a bit of a controversy over Father Bellis's daughter, who had, during one of our trips to Corona del Mar, taken it upon herself to get rebaptized without permission or without even telling anyone. Not too long after this, we got a call from a very angry Father Bellis.

"What's this I hear about my daughter getting rebaptized at Pirate's Cove?" he said sharply.

"Father Bellis, we had no idea she was planning on doing that. We're very sorry."

"Well, unfortunately it's the least of my concerns. If it were just my daughter I had to deal with, I wouldn't be too worried. But she's told all of her church friends about it, and now *they* want to be rebaptized too! What am I to do? This is not good. It has the potential to cause a lot of confusion and damage in our church."

The issue came to a point of such conflict that Father Bellis actually went to his bishop to ask for guidance. To his surprise, the bishop told him that rebaptism was permissible as long as it was reconfirming one's original baptismal vows, kind of like the way married couples renew their wedding vows.

Hearing that, Father Bellis wasn't angry with us anymore, thank goodness. And being totally at peace with the whole thing, he even started rebaptizing people himself.

So when Kurt and his wife, Debbie, came to Father Bellis about getting rebaptized, he said, "I'd be happy to baptize the both of you."

"Actually," Kurt said, "we were hoping *he* could baptize us," pointing at Fred. They thought since Fred was in charge of the Sunday night service that he was a priest too.

"Fred isn't a priest," Father Bellis said, "so he can't baptize you into the Episcopal Church. He can still baptize you, if you want, just not here in the church."

Well, this couple wasn't interested in becoming Episcopalians in the first place, so they told Father Bellis it didn't matter where they were baptized as long as it was Fred baptizing them.

Next, it was just a matter of figuring out where to baptize them. We had two choices: One of our church members was the director of the YMCA in Riverside, where there was a big heated pool—an important detail since it was late October and the weather had turned cold. The drawback of doing it there was that it was a public space, so there would be no guarantee of it being a distraction-free baptism. Our other option was at a parishioner's house pool. This would have the intimacy and privacy the YMCA lacked, but it wasn't heated.

"We'll feel more comfortable at the house pool," they said. "We don't mind a little cold water."

We scheduled the baptism for a Sunday afternoon. In the meantime, Fred was preparing a small exhortation to give to Kurt about being the spiritual leader of the home and the responsibilities that come with that role. He was very excited about conducting the baptism and about his sermon.

But when the day came and Fred tested the water, it was unbearably cold. Ice cold. Fred thought there was no way he'd be able to give a sermon in water that cold. His teeth would be chattering so hard the words would never get out.

"Maybe we should postpone and do it at the YMCA after all," Fred then suggested to Kurt.

"We're here now," Kurt said matter-of-factly. "Why don't we just jump in and you can baptize us real quick and then jump out?"

That meant Fred would have to scrap the sermon he had worked so hard on. However, realizing that their need to be baptized was more important than his sermon, Fred happily consented.

As Fred waded into the water with Kurt and his wife, it was so cold it took his breath away. He wasn't even sure he would have the strength or control to say, "I now baptize you in the name of the Father and of the Son and of the Holy Spirit," let alone anything else. Yet when he reached out to touch Kurt to pray over him, suddenly the pool turned as warm as bath water. It was a miracle! The water remained warm for the whole baptism, and Fred was able to give his sermon after all. In fact, when Fred and Kurt and Debbie all got out of the pool, their skin was pink from the stomach down. So it wasn't all in their heads; God literally changed the temperature of the water—another divine encounter.

Something else amazing happened during the baptism: As Kurt resurfaced from the water, being raised to new life, he was speaking in tongues! I'd never seen anything like that before. The same thing happened to Debbie.

We didn't know it at the time, but Kurt and Debbie had recently gotten into a discussion with someone about being baptized in the Holy Spirit, specifically about speaking in tongues. "You shouldn't get yourself involved in that kind of stuff," this person said. "It's not scriptural and can be dangerous." They were hearing the exact opposite at the Sunday night meetings at All Saints, though, and didn't know what to believe. In the time leading up to their baptism, they had been praying, "God, if the baptism of the Holy Spirit is real and right, we want to be baptized in the Holy Spirit at the same time as our water baptism," which is exactly what happened! Isn't that neat? That day was miracle after miracle.

Not long after this, Kurt and Debbie asked Fred if he could pray for them at one of our meetings. For many years they had been trying to have children, but with no success. After everything that had happened to them since that night at All Saints, they believed anything was possible with God.

The young people joined Fred and gathered around them to pray. Well, it should come as no surprise that not very long after they prayed, Kurt and Debbie found out they were pregnant with their first child. All in all, they had three children; they even have grandchildren now.

Kurt and Debbie are still walking with the Lord to this day. They eventually moved to Minnesota, where Kurt has a prison ministry. It's such a joy to see the fruit of people's salvation, especially when it has to do with those you've had some small part in bringing to the Lord.

But more than that, Fred and I feel extremely honored to have played a small role in the overall birthing of these Sunday evening meetings at All Saints Episcopal Church in Riverside, California, back in 1971. As you will see as our story continues, God had a much bigger plan than we could have ever imagined for these meetings, which actually became the very first Calvary Chapel transplant!

Fifteen

The Art of Trust

Ruth:

FRED AND I over the years have had the privilege of staying very connected with Lonnie Frisbee. From the time Fred was used by God to bring Lonnie up to Riverside, which resulted in an explosion of salvations and a move of the Holy Spirit among the youth of Southern California's Inland Empire, our home and our lives were wide open to him and his incredible ministry. He was literally always on the move, and you never knew when Lonnie would suddenly appear. In many ways he was in and out of our lives continually—but always in our hearts.

Lonnie often said that Chuck Smith trained him in the Word of God and Kathryn Kuhlman trained him in the Holy Spirit, but he eventually shared that he felt Fred and I were his true spiritual parents, since we were always there for him no matter what, through thick and thin. We walked with him from the time he was at the peak of his success at Calvary Chapel Costa Mesa, and we were there for him through a couple of extremely difficult seasons.

Speaking as a spiritual mom, I remember when Lonnie was very much misunderstood by many, used for his giftedness, or "thrown away" and written out of the church history books. I also remember the bitterness that tried to grab him. I told him one day, "Lonnie, don't worry. You will be receiving your full reward on the other side! God sees everything! You know that!"

But mostly I have very special memories of our times with Lonnie. He had such an endearing, fun personality, and he was so thoughtful and appreciative of everything, always bringing us gifts from far-away places. His childlike faith was both inspiring and challenging. I will always thank God for all the precious moments we shared with Lonnie right up until the end of his short life.

Back in Scandinavia

After about a year and a half into our Sunday evening meetings at All Saints, Lonnie felt called to join a ministry in Florida led by Bob Mumford and to continue his missionary journeys that he loved so much. Everyone was very disappointed here in our Riverside fellowship that Lonnie was leaving California. That was also true at Calvary Chapel Costa Mesa. However, God was not finished using Lonnie Frisbee—by far. To date, many books and films have been produced, documenting many of Lonnie's adventures (along with a few dramatic misadventures).

Shortly before Lonnie left for Florida, Fred and I joined him on a missionary trip to Scandinavia. Over the years Fred and I made multiple foreign trips with Lonnie, including to England, South Africa, and Brazil, where Lonnie made a huge impact. (You should read *Not by Might, Nor by Power*, authored by Lonnie himself with the help of his missionary friend Roger Sachs. This three-part series tells the whole story, and Fred wrote the introduction to part two, *The Great Commission*.)

We took twenty of our own kids from the Sunday night service, and about two hundred people from churches all over also went. Duane Pederson, the editor and founder of *The Hollywood Free Paper*, organized the whole thing. It was through his paper that he popularized the name "the Jesus People movement." His desire, and ours, was to bring the Jesus movement more fully to Scandinavia.

First we flew to Stockholm, Sweden, to gather with the whole group. What made this trip even more special from the start was that Father Bellis joined us. Before we had left the States, Father Bellis had exchanged pulpits with a priest from England. Since Sweden is just a hop, skip, and a jump from England, as far as plane rides go, Father Bellis was more than happy to participate; he had never done anything like that before.

From Stockholm everyone split into their original groups and went their own separate ways. Because of Fred's heritage, we took our team of twenty to Norway. Father Bellis stayed in Stockholm with a group from Phoenix. There was a Christian music group called the Sonshine that went to Finland.

We spent ten days in Norway in total, mostly doing street witnessing and visiting churches. A pastor from Oslo was our guide. One of the places I remember most was a city called Kristiansand, mainly because the Christians there were known as "Dark Christians," as they were a very serious and austere people. Like the Amish, they wore very plain, modest clothing; no jewelry or makeup for the women either. Their hymns were very serious and their services very formal and kind of depressing.

So when we showed up with a bunch of happy-go-lucky, California-sunshine kids from the Jesus movement, singing upbeat songs and wearing casual clothing, we caused quite a stir. As you know, our approach to God was "come like you are." And that's what we did, no matter where we were.

These Dark Christians thought we were the worst. We had a meeting at one of their churches, and well, they couldn't stand how informal, unstructured, and full of emotion it was. I mean, the first song we sang went something like, "Happy are the people whose God is the Lord"—nails on a chalkboard to them. Then during ministry time someone started speaking in tongues. (Afterward, Fred told me that, for the first time, he was certain God had given him an interpretation to tongues, but he was too afraid to speak it out given where we were. Someone else gave the interpretation instead, which was exactly what the Lord had given Fred.) One Dark Christian pulled a young leader from our group aside and told him, "You've got to get these people out of here." I'm not sure they thought we were even real Christians by this point, because we were so far from the Christianity they practiced.

Several of our kids also gave their testimonies. One young man talked about how harmful it was to condemn other Christians for the way they looked, how that was keeping a lot of people from Christ. He also talked about how the Christian life wasn't about rules, but about being in relationship with Christ. This was all pretty eye-opening and challenging for the Norwegians. They certainly put up a fight at first.

I can thankfully say that by the end of our stay in Kristiansand, the hearts of these Dark Christians, many of whom we were staying with in their homes, were softened to us and changed. "You have to forgive us," they said. "We realize now that you are Christians."

When all the teams returned to Stockholm, we visited a big park so that the kids could do some witnessing there. Drugs and drug-use were out in the open, which attracted a lot of young people to this park. It was the perfect place to send out an army of Spirit-filled, "on fire for Jesus" Christian young people. We adults were supposed to serve as overseers and let the kids do the witnessing, but I wanted to do something for the Lord.

I noticed a girl with a bunch of boys who were smoking pot; she was the only girl. I felt afraid for her. I knew in my heart, even without having talked to her yet, that these guys didn't have her best interest in mind, that they weren't really her friends. God put a burden on my heart to go share Jesus with her, to tell her about the friend she could have in him—the true friend, the one who laid his life down for her. I didn't want to approach her when she was with these guys, because I thought she might not open up with them around. So when she stepped away for a moment to go to a water fountain, I thought, *This is my chance!*

"Do you mind if I share something with you?" I asked, hoping she understood and spoke English.

"No, I don't mind," she said.

I told her everything God had placed on my heart for her: I warned her about drugs and that her friends over there were only dragging her down. I told her that Jesus loved her more than she could ever imagine; that only *he* had the best intentions for her; that she should listen to him more than anybody else because he died on the cross so she could know him and believe in him for everything. It was so exciting! I could tell I wasn't the one speaking to her—it was the Holy Spirit speaking through me. I then asked her if she wanted to accept Christ into her heart. And guess what? She did! She accepted Jesus into her heart right there—a wonderful divine encounter!

The next day Lonnie wanted to go back to the same park. "We've got to find that girl and see how's she's doing," he said to me. We found her working in this little refreshment stand in the park. Knowing this would most likely be the last time I ever saw her, I wanted to give her something to remember me by. Fred had bought me a little gold cross that I was wearing that day, and I felt like the Holy Spirit was telling me to give it to her. I said, "Honey, this necklace is a reminder of the commitment you made to Jesus yesterday. Please take it." She put the necklace on and thanked me. I'll never forget that! Lonnie was also so touched!

Fred has a similar story from that day in the park. While God was leading me to this girl, he led Fred over to a group of guys he was pretty sure were all high. He shared the Four Steps with them and then asked, "Is there any reason why you wouldn't like to receive Jesus as your Savior now?" Only one of the guys, who was on vacation from England, prayed with Fred to receive Christ that day—but one is always better than none.

Afterward, however, Fred started having doubts. Old smutty face Satan was putting in his head that it was all a sham: "Do you really think something happened with that young man today? You really think he believed all that? He was just being nice is all; he felt bad for you." Fred couldn't shake the thought. He left Stockholm full of doubt.

Fred and I traveled to Copenhagen next for a bit of vacation. He took me to the city's famous walking street first. Two years prior, Fred and a bunch of Jesus freak kids had prayed and witnessed there, and now Fred heard that the amount of pornography out in the open had gone down significantly since he had been there last. It was true! With most of the pornography gone, the walking street, with its coffee shops and boutiques and enchanting architecture, was one of the loveliest places I had ever been. It was like the place had been saved!

Anyway, during our walk, someone suddenly grabbed Fred's shoulder from behind, turning him around. It was kind of scary at first, but then we realized—it was that kid from the park in Stockholm!

"Do you remember me? Do you remember me?" he said with a great big smile.

"What are you doing here?" Fred asked, shocked and overjoyed to see him.

"I'm visiting Copenhagen before I go home to England. I saw you and just had to make sure it really was you. I wanted to tell you that since receiving Jesus, I've decided to take my rock band from London and travel around and play for Jesus! But first I have to save my bandmates!" The kid was just glowing with Jesus; there was no doubting his sincerity now.

What were the chances we would run into him again, in another city, in a different country? The odds were *huge*. Only God could have orchestrated this encounter—and just so Fred could be at peace about this young man. What a loving, compassionate God we have! Even when we fail to believe as we should, over and over, God still gives us grace, like a loving parent does. That moment on the walking street is a perfect example of God gently correcting Fred while at the same time blessing him. He reminded Fred, as he reminds us all every day, "You can trust in me."

Sixteen

A New Season

Fred:

FATHER BELLIS was a changed man when he returned to the States. Witnessing to kids in the parks and streets of Stockholm, collar off and all, seeing lives radically changed before his very eyes, really changed his perspective.

"Fred, I see now what I've been missing," he said to me not long after we got back. "If you wouldn't mind, I'd like to take over the Sunday night meetings. I need to be a part of what's going on." (Lonnie had gone to Florida by now and been replaced by Chuck Smith Jr.)

From the very beginning of our involvement at All Saints, Ruth and I had been trying to bring Father Bellis into a deeper, more dynamic relationship with the Holy Spirit; the whole reason we joined the Episcopal Church in the first place was because we saw it as a harvest field for the Lord. So, as surprised as I was, hearing Father Bellis tell me he wanted to take over the Sunday night meetings was music to my ears. I was more than happy to hand the reins over to him if that meant he was stepping into a greater anointing in the Holy Spirit.

But it wasn't as easy as all that. When I was in charge, I was pretty much the glorified greeter (and happy to be!). I was the guy giving all the kids big hugs as they came in. I prayed for them when they needed it. I was like an old hen trying to keep all her chicks safe in one place. I was actually driving myself a little crazy with that. I thought it was up to me keep all the kids in the faith. Then one day the Holy Spirit said to me, "You didn't save them; you can't keep them. That's my job. You just keep inviting them and loving them. Leave the rest to me." And so that's what I did.

Anyway, when I was in charge, I didn't get in the way of whatever Lonnie needed to do. I was most comfortable being behind the scenes, so to speak; the spotlight wasn't for me. That didn't mean I wasn't also present and fully committed to my role. I dearly loved each and every kid that came through those doors and did my best to let them know that. That was how I "led."

Father Bellis, on the other hand, had a hard time relating. He took a more hands-off, occasionally disciplinarian approach to his role. He'd begin most meetings with a little speech about keeping feet off of the kneelers and other proper conduct to abide by, and then he'd disappear into his office to work on his sermon for the upcoming Sunday. In other words, he didn't have the same love and concern for the All Saints kids that I had—and the kids noticed.

During this time, Lonnie came back from Florida and paid All Saints an unannounced visit. Unaware of the recent change in management, Lonnie walked into Father Bellis's office during one of the Sunday night meetings to say hello and to ask where I was. Father Bellis, however, being preoccupied with his work, mistook Lonnie for one of the kids and said rather coldly, "I thought I told you not to bother me when I'm in my office."

"Father Bellis . . . it's me . . . Lonnie."

"Lonnie! I'm so sorry. I thought you were the same kid that came in just a minute ago."

When Lonnie told me about this, it grieved me terribly and confirmed in my heart that I had made a mistake. I realized that it wasn't wise of me to have turned my ministry over to Father Bellis just because he asked it from me. This was especially true given that my ministry had been tailor-made for me by God. It took a certain kind of person to deal and relate with these teenagers. God had to pretty much break me beforehand to prepare me for this kind of work. Father Bellis, on the other hand, hadn't gone through the same trials; it was naive of me to assume he could relate to these kids the same way I could. He was a priest, not a youth pastor.

Meanwhile, Chuck Jr. stepped down from his position. That's when Lonnie, who would sort of blow in and out of our lives from here on out, brought Greg Laurie in as his replacement. At first I wasn't too enthusiastic about Greg: He was only eighteen, which I thought was a little too young, and to me, he came off as a little cocky. If it had been my decision, I would have chosen Kenn Gulliksen to take over, but he was unavailable. So Greg it was. And if Lonnie thought highly of him, then maybe Greg was worth a shot.

Well, turns out Lonnie was right. Greg was a perfect fit for All Saints. He was a gifted evangelist with a preaching style that was a potent mixture of Lonnie, Kathryn Kuhlman, and Bob Mumford. Greg also brought back the bands that Chuck Jr. had done away with. It wasn't long, then, until the church was packed out every Sunday evening like before. In the end, Greg was just as successful and beloved as Lonnie was—if not more. In the early days, when Lonnie was involved, the Lord showed me there would come a day when we would fill Landis Hall, the largest auditorium in Riverside at the time. That didn't end up happening when Lonnie was around, but after Greg came and built that place up again, that's exactly what they did. Later, when the city built the convention center in downtown Riverside, a much bigger facility than Landis Hall, they packed that place out too!

As for me and Ruth, we were still attending All Saints on Sunday mornings, but our involvement with the Sunday night meetings had officially ended when Father Bellis took over. I thought if I kept on going, I would end up interfering somehow. Naturally, though, I kept in touch.

I found out that with all their surging growth, the vestry at All Saints had become unhappy with the Sunday night meetings, which had been riding max capacity for a while; and with Father Bellis barely involved, things were getting a little out of hand. The Calvary group, for example, hadn't been doing their fair share of supporting themselves: It had become all take and no give. The vestry decided that Greg and company had outgrown their welcome and subsequently asked them to leave.

Of course, this was also falling on Father Bellis's head, exactly the thing he didn't want to have happen. Father Bellis came to me one day and said, "We need to do something about all these kids."

So I had a conference with Chuck Smith at Calvary Chapel Costa Mesa.

"All Saints isn't working for the kids anymore," I told him. "They need to have a total church experience; they need a place of their own."

Chuck agreed and eventually bought a defunct Baptist church on Arlington Ave. in Riverside. Greg was made head pastor, and the rest is history.

As you might have guessed, Greg eventually changed the name of his church to Harvest, which amazingly still meets at that same location, although now it's a megachurch. Today, Greg is a household name in the evangelical world, up there with the likes of Joel Olsteen, Rick Warren, and the late Billy Graham. Harvest is probably most famous for its Harvest Crusades ministry, which has been packing out stadiums around the world for decades.

Lonnie used to say that Harvest started in our living room at the Ranch, and in a way, he was right. We never had any afterglow meetings with Greg, but the ministry Greg inherited at All Saints owed a good deal of its existence to our afterglow meetings. I picture Harvest sometimes, with its thousands of people in attendance, or I think of Harvest Crusade and its tens of thousands of people, and I say to myself in amazement, "How is all that in any way connected to this—my home?" It's mind-boggling. Of course, it had nothing to do with me and Ruth in and of ourselves. It was all God. He took the seed and grew it into something beyond our imaginations. Which just goes to show you that God can do tremendous, world-changing things when you're faithful and humble with the little things.

A few years later Ruth and I left All Saints and began attending another Calvary church plant in Yorba Linda, where John Wimber was pastoring. We had heard some incredible things were happening there. I knew John from before and that he was a gifted preacher. More importantly, and perhaps not surprisingly, Lonnie was ministering there.

A couple years before this, John was at a Calvary Chapel pastors' retreat up in Big Bear in the mountains of Southern California. Out of nowhere Lonnie showed up and turned that place upside down with the power of the Holy Spirit. Grown men were on the floor, weeping or laughing. Lonnie had led most of these guys to the Lord earlier in their lives, and now they were getting touched by God and being healed—including John. When it was all over, John said to Lonnie, "You gotta come speak at my church."

From that point on John had Lonnie stick close by. He was aware of the recent wounds Lonnie had suffered from people high-up in ministry. John felt it was important to restore Lonnie to his former office, as he was far too gifted and anointed not to have church backing.

One day, while John and Lonnie were having lunch together, Lonnie brought up the Calvary Chapel in Riverside. "I had a part in starting that church," he told John. "It all started in Fred Waugh's house, actually. He's the one who brought me to Riverside."

"You know Fred Waugh?" John asked, amazed.

"Yeah, I know Fred. Why?"

Let me back up some years—to 1962. When my business partner and I split up, I ended up with the office building. Because I no longer needed a building of that size, I subleased the back part of my building to a credit union. Our two companies shared a receptionist, who was brought over from the credit union. Her name was Candy Tuttle.

Candy was pregnant, but there was a problem: Her Mormon boyfriend didn't want to marry her, because Candy wasn't Mormon. I had shared Christ with her early on in our relationship and even agreed to co-counsel her and her boyfriend with his stake president in the Mormon Church. I think Candy needed someone there at the sessions who better represented her interests in the matter; otherwise the meetings would have been pretty one-sided.

As I continued to witness to Candy, one day she said to me, "Fred, you need to meet these two guys from the credit union. They sound just like you!" Their names were John Wimber and Dick Heinz, both of whom had previously been with the Righteous Brothers before converting to Christianity and consequently were in need of new work.

When I met them, naturally I asked if they had been baptized in the Holy Spirit.

"What's the baptism of the Holy Spirit?" they asked.

They seemed open and interested, so I walked them through the pertaining Bible verses and then shared with them my own personal testimony.

"Do you mind if I pray for you both to receive the Holy Spirit?"

"Please do," they said.

I prayed—and just like that, John Wimber and Dick Heinz were speaking in tongues, in the middle of a workday, inside my office. You never know where God might take you when you walk in the Spirit. The most ordinary of days can be turned extraordinary; everyday life can be marked by divine encounters.

Later that same day John took a walk by himself in an orange grove next to his house. Apparently, he had an overwhelming God-experience while praying, which confirmed in his heart what had happened in my office was for real. This led to John and his wife, Carol, coming to our Bible study. I remember John being very open and warm; Carol, on the other hand, who hadn't experienced what her husband had, was overall skeptical of the whole thing. Both she and John were members of the Friends Church in Yorba Linda, an evangelical Quaker church that didn't affirm the baptism of the Holy Spirit as a second, separate impartation of grace, nor believe in practicing the gifts of the Holy Spirit. When Carol went to her pastor with this new family development, naturally he said, "All that speaking in tongues stuff—that's of the devil," which spooked John and Carol. They stopped attending our Bible study, and for the most part, I lost all contact with him. Sadly, John walked away from the Holy Spirit and renewed his commitment to his Quaker roots.

Nonetheless, John was used powerfully by God at the Friends Church in Yorba Linda. He began leading people to the Lord left and right, his church growing like crazy. In fact, John became such a notable soul winner in his area, Fuller Theological Seminary hired him to work in their church growth department. They sent him to churches all over the country, sharing church growth principles and methods. He did this for a number of years.

After a while, though, it started to wear on him—not just the traveling, but more so the nature of his work. He was tired of obstinate pastors who were more concerned with building their own "kingdoms" than they were in helping build the kingdom of God. He was tired of presenting church models and giving sound advice that wasn't appreciated or taken seriously.

It all came to a head one night while John was alone in his hotel in Chicago. John was totally burnt out and depressed. Desperate, he fell flat on his face and cried out to the Lord, "God, this can't be right. I can't do this anymore. What am I doing wrong? What's missing?" The Holy Spirit then responded to him gently, "When you rejected the Holy Spirit at the Waughs' Bible study, you turned your back on me."

John was beside himself in grief.

"Forgive me, forgive me!" he cried out.

It was a dramatic turning point in John Wimber's life that would totally change the trajectory of his ministry and walk with the Lord.

John tried getting hold of me when he got back to California, but because I was attending Melodyland School of Theology, it was somewhat difficult to reach me in those days. Whenever I tried calling back, I could never reach John. We played phone tag like that for a bit until the idea of reconnecting was either dropped or forgotten.

Meanwhile, John quit his job at Fuller in pursuit of ministry that reflected his rediscovered beliefs in the Holy Spirit. He was soon after contacted by Candy Tuttle, our former joint receptionist, who asked him if he would be interested in starting a Bible study in her home. That Bible study, which John agreed to take on, eventually became Calvary Chapel Yorba Linda, which brings us back to the pastors' conference in Big Bear.

Calvary Chapel Yorba Linda was meeting in a high school gym when Lonnie reappeared on the scene and first spoke there. That was the Mother's Day service in 1980 that virtually birthed a new movement of God that eventually went worldwide. As Lonnie yelled, "Holy Spirit, come," literally hundreds of young people were simultaneously knocked to the gymnasium floor, many uncontrollably crying, others laughing or speaking in tongues, pinned to the floor for what seemed like an eternity. This was another earth-shattering, horizons-expanding experience for John that sent him home reeling, wondering how to process it all and how in the world to move forward.

Well, as the story goes, the Mother's Day phenomenon caused John to develop his ministry with an emphasis on the Holy Spirit. As much as this "Holy Spirit led" way of doing church unnerved John, he couldn't deny its power and potential to bring about true change in the world for God's kingdom. People were being healed, getting saved, being baptized in the Holy Spirit, and seeing God move in dramatic, awe-inspiring fashion; it felt like God was in their midst like never before.

The history of the early Vineyard could be a couple books in itself, but by 1980 there were already seven Vineyards under the banner of Kenn Gulliksen in the LA/Beverly Hills area reaching people in the entertainment, music, and sports industries. Several of the congregations went well into the thousands. Bill Dwyer and Keith Green both came to prominence in these early Vineyards. Kenn and his wonderful wife, Joanie, had a longstanding relationship and history with Lonnie Frisbee and John Wimber several years prior to Mother's Day and even considered Calvary Chapel Yorba Linda a "sister church" to the Vineyard. After the controversial Mother's Day service and subsequent change in emphasis on spiritual gifts from Calvary Chapel's more conservative teaching-focused one, Kenn approached John and offered him to come under the Vineyard umbrella. He also felt John was more of a "pastor to the pastors" than he and turned over that area of leadership also.

So John changed the name of his church to the Anaheim Vineyard Christian Fellowship for what would become a new church movement as dozens of Calvary Chapels also became Vineyards. The Vineyard went from seven churches to over forty almost overnight, and now number well over two thousand worldwide.

John Wimber brought Lonnie on staff in his church right away. For the next three years they were a powerful team, and Lonnie used his missionary connections to open the nations up to the Vineyard. Lonnie said, "I brought a move of the Holy Spirit back from South Africa in 1980, and John Wimber took it around the world." They formed Vineyard teams going to England, Europe, Israel, South Africa, and other destinations. Lonnie took teams to South America and to one of his very favorite countries, Brazil, every year from 1978 onward. John Wimber and Lonnie took a large Vineyard team of a hundred on one trip to South Africa alone.

After Lonnie brought up my name to John Wimber, we finally reconnected. Ruth and I then began attending and getting involved at John's church. Just as we had at All Saints, we invited the youth of the Vineyard to the Ranch for weekly meetings that John Wimber attended as well. The Ranch was the Vineyard's first Riverside kinship location (prior to John, Kenn called his home groups "kinships"), which was an outreach program Wimber developed.

We also went on a couple of mission trips with John and Lonnie over the course of the next few years. The first was to England. One of the more significant stories from that trip took place in an English village not too far outside of London called Chorleywood, where we had a meeting at a small, quaint Anglican church. St. Andrew's was packed that night, mostly with young people. Ruth and I had seats near the back. A little old lady in a wheelchair was sitting next to us alongside the outside aisle.

When John and Lonnie gave the altar call and all these people were walking up either to accept Christ or to be filled with the Holy Spirit, Ruth and I could tell the lady next to us wanted to go up too, but it was too crowded for her to make it up there in her wheelchair. Ruth said to her, "Honey, you know what—they are not the healer. Jesus is the healer. And Jesus can heal you right here if you want."

The lady told us she had MS, which hit home because our daughter suffered from the same disability. This "coincidence" only served to confirm that we were supposed to pray for her, so Ruth asked if she could.

"Sure, you can pray for me" the elderly woman said.

"Lord Jesus," Ruth prayed, "I pray you heal this woman from MS and give her the strength to walk again!"

Next, Ruth took her by the hands, lifted her slowly to her feet—and the woman walked! People had to make way for her as she went up and down the aisles, pushing her wheelchair from behind. The meeting was taken to the next level of rapture and joy. Some people were even standing on their pews so that they could see what was going on. It was a small town, so everyone knew this woman and about her *former* condition.

For me, seeing that woman healed was both awe-inspiring and difficult at the same time. As happy as I was for her, I couldn't help but think of my daughter, Linda. I couldn't tell you how many times we had prayed for her to be healed of MS, but for whatever reason, God hadn't healed her. Why? I suppose we don't have the luxury of knowing such answers.

But in a way I already had my answer: Linda's body certainly suffered because of her disease; she lost just about all of her bodily freedom and was bound to a wheelchair. On top of that, her husband divorced her. She could have easily become bitter, even hateful toward God and the cruelty of life. Yet all of that suffering only served to strengthen the life of God in her. Amazingly, the question of *why*—as a complaint—never fell from her lips. If the topic of her condition was ever brought up, she'd always say, "I have a choice: I can grow bitter or better." Linda wanted to be better; she wanted to be kinder; she wanted to be more beautiful on the inside, even if that beauty seemed to reflect less and less in her physical appearance.

It's only natural that when we suffer, we want to remove ourselves from that suffering as soon as possible or at the very least find someone or something to blame for that suffering. But Jesus embraced his suffering and defeated it, not by running from it, but by transforming it as a means of growing closer to God and others. Linda did the same: She followed Christ *through* her MS. She showed everyone that MS had no power over her will to live and love, that it had no power to make her feel any less than she knew herself to be in Christ. She defeated MS by turning it into a blessing. "I am so blessed," she said *all the time*; it's even on her tombstone, which she requested before she died.

Now, I can't say for certain why God didn't heal her in this life. What I do know, however, is that she is healed *now*, and that she was living proof of a life well-lived and well-loved, not only despite her disease, but because of it.

Linda Rae Waugh

I never felt closer to Linda than I did during those difficult years, and for that I am thankful. MS cut her life short—and that's a tragic thing in and of itself—but in no way did it diminish or rob her of the years that she did have. Linda was an angel. And what more should you want from your children than for them to become angels while on the earth?

South Africa

A year or so after our trip to England, Ruth and I took another short mission trip with the Vineyard to South Africa. About fifty people were on that team, including John and Lonnie. This had to be about 1982.

We flew into Johannesburg. The first home we stayed in was a big Dutch home, of all places. Apartheid was still in full effect, so blacks and whites were totally segregated, a terribly sad thing to see. The team split into two groups: Lonnie in our group and John in the other (but just like Lonnie, John went off and did his own thing most of the time). On one occasion, Lonnie took off to a part of town that was all black. He preached out there and had some amazing results. He was fearless when it came to evangelism.

Ruth and I, on the other hand, played it safe. We kept to the safe parts of town and shared at churches that were on the schedule. One day Ruth and I were walking down this street in Johannesburg, when suddenly a stranger stopped us, warning us that we were in a dangerous part of town and shouldn't be wearing our backpacks on our backs. "Wear them in front of you," he said. "No one will steal from you then." Apparently, it was common for the backpacks of tourists to be snatched right off their backs or cut open with a razor. *Yikes!* We had no idea. We thanked the stranger and did as he instructed.

"Do you think he was an angel?" Ruth asked once the man was gone.

"He could have been," I said. "Either way, God was looking out for us."

When we left Johannesburg for Cape Town, we teamed up with a Methodist superintendent who oversaw twelve churches in the area. After a prayer meeting that we had at his home church, he asked if we would go with him to meet and pray for several of his parishioners at their homes, which we were more than happy to do. It was an amazing experience. We visited several homes that day. We prayed for a man who was an alcoholic, and God healed him on the spot. It was so beautiful. We baptized several people in the Spirit, some of whom also committed their lives to the Lord, even though they were already professing Christians in the Methodist Church. Unfortunately, many mainstream denominations tend to reduce Christianity to going to church on Sunday or to just living the moral life. People think that as long as they do enough good, or more aptly put, that as long as they don't do too much bad, they will go to heaven when they die. So many of the folks that we met in Cape Town had very little understanding or experience of what it meant to have a personal relationship with Christ and even less of an idea of the importance of receiving the Holy Spirit. But there's not much else in this world that excites me more—and gets me talking!—than sharing the gospel and the reality of the Holy Spirit with people, Christian or not.

As an aside, we got to stay in a women's Catholic monastery during our time in Cape Town. Now, I don't think they were Spirit-filled Catholics, at least as far as I could tell, but every morning and night we could hear the nuns singing from our room. It was the most beautiful singing, like a heavenly choir!

All in all, we spent about three weeks in South Africa and had some amazing experiences. And this was all because of Lonnie. He's the one who opened the door for us to go. Moreover, that trip and others established the Vineyard in South Africa, which became its first international church plant. Now they have multiple churches in that country; in fact, there are now Vineyards in almost all African countries. It's amazing to think that Ruth and I had a small part in what God did and is still doing on the entire African continent. Praise God!

Seventeen
Heavenly Blessings

Fred:

ON OUR WAY home from South Africa, we had a three-day layover in Brazil. Ruth and I did our own thing while Lonnie ricocheted about doing ministry stuff, as was his way. Just prior to this, however, during our flight, Lonnie asked if I could help find him a new car, reminding me that he had sold his previous car in order to finance his trip. Knowing I was friends with a dealer back in Riverside, Lonnie asked, "Maybe you could help me get a good deal on something." I said I'd be happy to help.

As soon as I got back home, I started brainstorming. At the time I had a '79 GM diesel pickup truck, the first of its kind. (This was during the gas crisis of the late seventies and early eighties, when some of the car companies were venturing into diesel.) I got pretty good gas mileage out of my '79 truck. Better yet, I had my own diesel tank at the Ranch, since I had diesel tractors of my own, which was really convenient when it came time to filling up. Instead of sitting in line for hours at the gas station during the gas shortage, which had led to gas prices skyrocketing, I could buy four thousand gallons of diesel (at fifteen cents a gallon!) and avoid the gas stations almost altogether.

However, as I would later find out, the conversion rate in my truck wasn't all that it was cracked up to be. The model started having some minor problems over time because it was built to utilize diesel fuel in a gasoline-designed engine. In other words, diesel was proving to be too powerful for the engine. So when General Motors announced that they were coming out with a new diesel truck, designed from scratch, I thought to myself, *Man, I'd really like to have one of those.*

In the meantime, as I was coming home from Orange County one day, the Holy Spirit spoke to me, saying, "Lonnie still needs a car. Why don't you buy yourself one of these new diesel trucks and give Lonnie the truck you have now?" *That's an idea!* My '79 only had ten to fifteen thousand miles on it; it was practically new, and I hadn't had any significant problems with it other than that the conversion rate wasn't too great.

This could work, I thought optimistically.

At the same time, buying a brand-new truck to replace a practically new one wasn't the most practical of decisions, nor would it be cheap. My '79 was probably worth $7,500—a pretty big sum of money in those days. Was there a better, less expensive option I hadn't thought of yet?

But then the Holy Spirit replied, "Just go check it out."

So I went down to the Chevrolet garage as soon as I could to see what my chances were of getting one of these new diesel trucks.

"Oh man, you know, it'd be a couple of years at least before you could get one of those," the dealer said. "We could put one on back order for you, but like I said, you wouldn't get it for years, most likely."

Lonnie can't wait years for a car, I thought. I took the news as a sign that maybe I hadn't heard the Holy Spirit quite like I thought I had. It was back to the drawing board.

Around Thanksgiving, during one of our meetings at the Ranch, I received a call from the director of Young Life. (I knew the director quite well because Ruth and I had been supporting his ministry for years.) He said, "Fred, I just wanted to call you and see if you would be interested in entering our upcoming raffle for a brand-new Pontiac 6000." A light went on in my head: *This is God's answer! This is how I get Lonnie's car!* I was sure of it. I was going to win this car, no doubt about it!

"The drawing takes place just before Christmas," he added.

"Perfect! I'll take two tickets!" I said loud enough for everyone to hear. "I'm going to win that thing!" (Don't ask why I bought two tickets when I only needed one. I'm sure I had a good reason at the time.) "Oh, and don't put them in my name, put them under Lonnie Frisbee."

"Okay, Fred. Lonnie Frisbee it is."

Once I got off the phone, I explained to everyone about the call and that I was going to win that car. I said that this was God's answer to Lonnie's need. Everyone was like, "Okay, Fred. If you say so." Now, this wasn't my normal self; I've always been pretty "realistic." I was never one of those "name it and claim it" kind of Christians. I'm still not. Nor have I ever considered myself the prophetic type. Simply put, it's not my gift. But for some reason this was different. Somehow I *knew*—and there was no convincing me otherwise.

A couple of weeks later, however, I got another call from the Young Life director, this time with a bit of bad news: "Fred, I hate to tell you this, but we didn't sell enough tickets to pay for the car, so we're going to have to postpone the raffle until Valentine's Day."

I was pretty disappointed. Although all was not lost, it felt like strike two, nonetheless. But Valentine's Day it would have to be, which unfortunately meant Lonnie would have to be without a car for another two months.

Meanwhile, later that month, Ruth and I had a large group of South Africans over for dinner, mostly young people we had met during our recent trip. Ruth was preparing the meal, when she discovered we were out of milk and asked if I could run to the store quickly to get some. Like a good husband, I said, "Sure, honey," but just as I was about to walk out the door, the phone rang. It was the Chevrolet dealership.

"Hey, Fred," the dealer said, "I just got that new diesel pickup in the garage—the one you were interested in."

"You don't say," I said. "I thought you said you wouldn't be getting any of those for a while?"

"Well, a guy who ordered the truck couldn't complete the deal, so now it's sitting here if you want to come take a look at it."

Being the judicious man that I was, I thought, *I'll just take a quick look and then get the milk. It won't take long.* Well, to make a long story short, I didn't come home with milk—but I did have a slip that said I was now the owner of a brand-new diesel truck! I think Ruth was more confused than upset when I explained to her what happened; under most circumstances a good wife would have given her husband the scolding of a lifetime—coming home with a car instead of milk. Thank God I have such an understanding wife: She knew how important finding a car for Lonnie was to me.

The next day we picked up the new truck and brought it home. I had it all planned out: I'd give my old truck a good polish, wrap it in a big ribbon, and surprise Lonnie with it on Christmas Day, which had been my plan all along with the Pontiac, until that had fallen through.

Then my older brother, Eric, who lived a couple of towns over, showed up at my house out of the blue. He pulled up in his old beat-up Datsun truck that he had used for years in construction before he retired due to disability; now he was using it for an early morning paper route he was running to supplement his disability income.

"Why do you have two trucks in your driveway?" he asked me.

Honestly, I didn't want to tell him the truth. I was ashamed that I hadn't thought of my own brother's need for a new truck until I saw him that day.

"What do you plan on doing with the old truck?" he asked after I told him both trucks were mine. "I could really use it. Mine's falling apart, you know."

Well, I had to tell the truth: "I'm so sorry, Eric, but I already promised it to someone else."

"Who?"

I wasn't sure how much it would help my case, but I told him about Lonnie, how he sold his car to finance his trip to South Africa and asked me personally to help him find a new car when we got back to the States.

"I've been trying to find him a car ever since," I said.

Not being a Christian, Eric took it just about the way I thought he would: "I get it," he said, and I could hear the hurt and resentment in his voice.

For the next couple of days I was pretty depressed about letting my brother down. Eric's life had been somewhat of a mess, and for some time. He was a struggling alcoholic; he'd been married four or five times, with his current marriage on the brink of another divorce, and he had financial struggles to go with all that. If only there were a way I could rectify his vehicle situation to help lighten his load a bit.

And then I remembered the raffle tickets.

If I win that Pontiac, I thought, *I could give it to Eric instead. Problem solved!*

Straightaway I called up Young Life and told them to change the name on the tickets from Lonnie to my brother's name. Then I called Eric to tell him the future good news.

"Don't worry," I said, "I'll have a new car for you by Valentine's Day."

"You will? How?"

"I know this is going to sound crazy, but I entered a raffle for a brand-new Pontiac 6000 a few weeks back—and I *know* I'm going to win it."

"How could you possibly know that? Is it rigged or something?"

"No, no. Nothing like that. I just have a good feeling about it. I can't explain."

"Yeah, sure, Fred. Thanks a lot," he said sarcastically.

He'll see, I said to myself after we got off the phone.

Eric, however, who understandably didn't share my confidence one bit, went out and financed a new truck for himself without telling me. When I found out, my heart deflated: To add to all my brother's money troubles, now he had a car payment, for which I felt partially responsible. What was I to do now? I couldn't go back on my word to Lonnie. And what was I supposed to do with the Pontiac if I did win it? I was in a no-win situation. Strike three—you're out!

Why was I so certain I would win that car in the first place? I thought dispiritedly. *Where did that feeling come from if it wasn't from God?*

All my doubting prompted me to take a closer look at the terms and conditions of the raffle. I discovered something that brought a chink of light back into my darkening predicament. I read that the winner of the car had two options: accept the car at a market value of $10,000 or accept $7,500 in cash. *That's it! That's my saving grace!* If there was anything that Eric needed, it was cash to help him pay off his new truck.

And just like that, my confidence was restored. Still, though, I would have to wait a couple of months for the drawing to take place. In the meantime, I was praying no more curveballs came my way; the situation was complicated enough as it was.

Valentine's Day came, and we were in the middle of another house meeting when I got a call from the Young Life director about the results of the raffle drawing. This was the moment of truth. There were about thirty or forty kids at the meeting that night, all dead silent, waiting eagerly to see my reaction.

"Fred, I can't believe I'm saying this," my director friend said. "You won the car!"

Everyone went crazy when they heard I had won.

"I told you I would win!" I said ecstatically.

"You did, you did!" they were saying. "We can't believe it!"

I called Eric right away. He was speechless. He was in shock.

"I didn't win the car," I reminded him. "*You* won it. And I don't mean to rub it in, you know, but if you hadn't gone out and bought that truck, you would have a brand-new car to your name—and for free!"

Of course, there was still the cash-out option, which I told him about.

"How much in cash?" he asked.

"Seven thousand, five hundred dollars."

"I don't believe it!" he said with even greater shock than before. "I owe seven thousand on my truck!"

Unbelievable! I thought. *This was what all those twists and turns were about!*

"Isn't God just amazing?" I said. "And you have five hundred to spare! What a deal!"

I was over the moon for my brother. But above all else, I was beyond thankful to the Lord for his care and provision. It was a bit of a wild ride, but worth it in the end. Little did I know, the best part of this ride was yet to come.

A few days later I got a call from Eric.

"Fred, I got to thinking: I really feel like I ought to tithe on the money we won."

Now, like I said, Eric wasn't a Christian, but having been raised in a Christian home, he knew tithing was the right thing to do. Plus, I was pretty sure God had reawakened something in him through all of this.

"I think that's a mighty good idea," I said.

Then he said, "I just thought maybe you'd have some idea where I ought to give the money."

"Why don't you give it to Young Life, as a way of saying thank you."

"That's a good idea; I hadn't thought of that. Maybe we could give half to Young Life and the other half to a pastor that I know from my paper route. We can give it to his little church."

"Why him?" I asked out of curiosity.

"Last Christmas, while I was delivering papers, this pastor came out of his house at four in the morning to wish me Merry Christmas and to give me a box of candy. That really meant a lot to me. And, well, he's been talking to me about God ever since, actually, trying to get me to come to his church. I've told him, 'No, thanks. Religion's not for me,' so many times. But the man doesn't take no for an answer, and neither does his kindness."

"That sounds great," I said. "God gave you the money—I think you should be the one to decide how to tithe it."

So he gave me a check to give to Young Life, and the other half he set aside for this pastor and his church.

Eric tried calling the church first, but he couldn't get hold of anyone. So then he drove down to the church one weekday evening. When he knocked on the doors, someone he'd never met before answered. Eric could see that the church was in the middle of a meeting of some kind. He was let in.

"Eric! What a pleasant surprise to see you this evening," said the pastor. "What brings you here?"

"Well, you've been trying to get me to come to your church," Eric said, "so I thought I'd stop by and check it out. I hope I'm not interrupting something important."

"Oh, we're just having a board meeting about what to do with our broken air conditioning and furnace. We were praying about what to do since we don't have the money to fix them, when you showed up."

"If you don't mind my asking, what would it take to fix them?"

"Three hundred and fifty dollars," he said.

"Did you say three hundred and fifty dollars?"

"I did. Why?"

Eric showed him the money. "I came to give you and your church this: It's three hundred and fifty dollars."

Needless to say, everyone that night was blown away, especially Eric, and when he told us, Ruth and I were blown away too! God was just blowing everyone away with these divine encounters. What filled my heart with more joy than anything else was that, as a result of all this, my brother committed his life to Christ!

When my mom heard, she was on cloud nine. Out of all of her children, she worried most about Eric because his life had been the most tragic; he was her prodigal son. But now he was back, and in the best of ways—back in the arms of the Lord. He was happy again, going to church again; he even became the Sunday school teacher at that little church he had donated to and remained there until he passed at the age of seventy-five.

Thinking back, I originally thought Eric winning the money was the happy ending I was hoping for; I thought it was the reason this whole series of events started in the first place. I never would have guessed that my promise to help Lonnie find a new car would have ended with my brother's salvation—the greatest divine encounter. What wisdom! What power! I can't help but believe that this was God's plan all along. I mean, what's a couple of new cars compared to one person's eternal destiny?

Whereas my intention was earthly blessing, God's was a heavenly, eternal blessing. This isn't to say we *shouldn't* bless people materially when they're in need, but rather that we should have the confidence that through our meager attempts to bless people in love, God can and will sanctify these works for his eternal purposes. Like it illustrates in Matthew 25, our acts of compassion and kindness to others are done to Christ himself and will be remembered in the end of all things. Even the smallest work of generosity, offered to God in love and worship, God can do infinitely with.

I don't know how many people God has blessed through all of this or how many more will be blessed by the sharing of this story. Regardless, I rest assured that God is on the move. He is at work saving lives *through our weaknesses* because that's how his power is made known!

Eighteen
A Simple Prayer

Fred:

I'VE HAD THE privilege of working with a number of Christian universities over the years. First was ORU, which I've talked about at some length already. The next university I became involved with was Southern California Bible College, which later became Vanguard University.

In 1975, I enrolled in some Bible courses at Melodyland School of Theology, just for my own edification. I wasn't thinking about further education or anything like that. Prior to enrolling, I came across a list of some courses and thought, *A class on Romans? A class on learning ancient Greek? Wouldn't that be fun!* So I went down to the registrar's office to inquire if I could audit the classes; I wasn't interested in the strain of all the homework and testing and what have you. But they told me they didn't allow people to audit, because of high dropout rates. "If you want to take classes," they said, "you'll have to enroll."

"Sign me up, then," I said. *What could be the harm?*

Well, I enjoyed my semester so much, I went ahead and enrolled the following semester too. I met John Ruttkay during this time, and we became really good friends. He was in the same boat as me—taking courses purely out of interest. We were doing so well in our studies and enjoying ourselves so much, together we came to the conclusion that we might as well go through the school's two-year program and earn our diplomas. "That would be a good thing for us to have," I said, "since we're both involved in ministries of our own."

So that's what we did. However, just before I earned my diploma, Melodyland's financial problems came to a head. Most of our professors were moonlighting from Southern California Bible

College; so when it was all but certain Melodyland was going under, SCBC stepped in and offered to accept credits toward a degree of their own.

I had no intention of transferring credits, but then a friend at Melodyland, who had the goal of becoming a priest, asked me, "What do I do?"

"You need to take advantage of this offer. Why don't you go down there and check it out. You could end up with a theology degree from an accredited school."

"Well, why don't you come with me?" he said.

I couldn't think of a good reason not to go with him, so I did. I was quite impressed by what I saw and got to thinking, *Why not go all the way and get my degree?* So my friend and I, along with John Ruttkay, transferred to Southern California Bible College.

Now that I was getting my degree, I had to make up some of the general education courses through community college. I hadn't been in public school for thirty years, so to get back in the classroom and compete with kids fresh out of high school was quite the struggle. But I worked my tail off and managed most of my courses. I finished all my coursework in 1979 and graduated from SCBC in May of 1980 with a degree in biblical studies, which for a fifty-some year old was quite an accomplishment.

That whole experience gave me a greater appreciation for education and the sacrifices one has to make in order to succeed as a student, not to mention the cost, which I had been well aware of since my days at ORU. Being in business for myself, however, and having a very successful career of my own allowed me to pay my way through higher education; I didn't have to subsidize my education like most (younger) students had to. So I thought, *You know, tuition alone doesn't cover the cost of a degree. You've got all of these other expenses on top of that, like books and food and what have you. Why don't I make a donation to help out?* And, well, when you make a substantial donation to any institution, you end up becoming involved with them from then on out. Subsequently, I was put on SCBC's donor list and have been supporting them ever since, and I've been on a first-name basis with all of the school's presidents since our initial donation.

Now, as an Assemblies of God institution, SCBC firmly believed in the baptism of the Holy Spirit and the gifts, but when I was attending, I noticed the faculty tended to downplay the fullness of the Spirit. They weren't denying the gifts, in particular speaking in tongues, but they had sort of relegated them to the back room, to the archives, so to speak, for the fear of bad press. For them, it was more of a historical event rather than a current reality. That was the impression I got anyway. Just my opinion.

In any case, God really impressed upon my heart to do what I could to help Vanguard (the university's new name) return to its Pentecostal roots. With the relationship I had with the Vanguard's faculty, God gave me a platform to have a loving, frank discussion concerning the gifts of the Holy Spirit.

Today they're as open as ever about the gifts. Mike Beals, their current president and my good friend, has had a lot to do with the revitalization of Vanguard's original position on the baptism of the Holy Spirit. I'm happy to have been a part of that.

Another university I've had the privilege of working with is Biola, but in order to fully tell that story and its significance, I have to go back to 1961, not long after Ruth and I returned from our trip around the world. At this time I was a brand-new born-again Christian and really struggling with prayer (this was before I was speaking in tongues). At one of our very early Bible studies, Carl Cook (the missionary friend of mine in Mexico who sold the Ichthys decals) told me to set aside a time every day for prayer and for reading the Scriptures—preferably in the morning, if possible. I said I'd do my best.

It just so happened that on early weekday mornings, Ruth drove Linda to the Christian high school she was attending in Paramount, which gave me about an hour or more to myself at home before I had to head out to work. I decided I'd use some of that time to pray and read the Bible, like my friend Carl had suggested. Reading the Bible was easy enough, but praying I found an extremely uphill battle. I tried praying silently, but my mind was full of distractions and competing thoughts. Like flies buzzing around my ears, thoughts of the day, of work ahead, or just random thoughts from seemingly nowhere made it impossible to concentrate. Most of my prayer time was spent trying to swat these stubborn "flies" away. By the end of my prayer time I felt frustrated and defeated. I remember thinking to myself, *I don't think this is the way prayer is supposed to work, nor do I think this is how I should feel when I do it.*

The next time I saw Carl, I expressed my frustration to him.

"I struggle with that myself," he said. "But one thing that I've found helpful is praying out loud."

Even alone, praying out loud sounded uncomfortable, but I knew personal prayer was vital to the Christian life, so I was willing to try it.

I quickly discovered that praying out loud *did* help with my level of concentration, but it also came with its own challenges. The struggle of prayer wasn't so much a matter of concentration now, but of power and effectiveness. It felt like my spoken prayers didn't have the strength to make it beyond the ceiling, like rockets with not nearly enough fuel to get to their destination. This was partly because I felt very self-conscious praying out loud. On top of that, thinking about what to pray for was difficult enough. The prayers I did manage to say out loud sounded pathetic to me, which made me feel pathetic inside. Soon enough I was just as disheartened, if not more, as before, when I was praying silently. But I kept at it.

One time as I was praying, thoughts about work crept in, as per usual. This time, instead of fighting them, I just went along. *I don't have any new projects to work on today,* I suddenly thought. Before my rational mind could catch up with what I was feeling, I was asking

God, "Could you lead me to a piece of property today? I have nothing to work on."

Immediately I felt foolish for asking for such a thing. *Who do YOU think you are? You think God listens to petty prayers like that? Doesn't he have better things to do than help you with your day job?*

Later that morning, I went to the Anaheim Savings and Loan, where I was arranging a construction loan on behalf of Christian Center (later Melodyland). Christian Center was meeting at the Anaheim Women's Assistance League building at the time, but this new loan would financially allow them to build a new church facility on a three-acre parcel right by the freeway in Anaheim. On my way out I bumped into a former real estate salesman from when Vernon and I were partners.

"Fred! How ya been? Long time no see! Is it true what I've heard about you?" referring to my recent conversion to Christianity, which he had heard about through the grapevine.

"It's true," I said.

"Wow," he said. "Pretty amazing stuff. So what are you doing these days?"

"Well, I'm working with a friend of mine. We're putting service station corners together."

"You don't say," he said. "Hey, I've got a piece of property you might be interested in. On Main Street in front of St. Joseph's Hospital."

The Holy Spirit suddenly said to me, "Wake up, Fred. This is it."

"I'm interested," I said.

The property was a small strip center with two hundred feet of frontage on Main St. Its focal point was a Spanish-styled building built around 1929, just before the big crash. It was a well-made, steel-framed structure. After the Depression, a good deal of the original Spanish architecture had been covered over or replaced with modern-looking, cheaper-quality add-ons, but it was still a nice building. The rest of the strip, however, was kind of a misfit, post-Depression development: There was a junky beer bar and a pet store in the back, a party supply store, and some apartments up on the second floor. The place was kind of a dump but had potential. I was definitely interested.

"Only problem is," my friend then went on to say, "there are about fourteen tenants on the property and the existing owner wants only one tenant to make it easier to manage."

Oh boy, I thought. I'd been in situations like this before—and very rarely did they work out.

And you thought this was the property God was leading you to, a mocking voice suddenly said in my head.

"Tell you what," I said, "when you got all your ducks in a row, stop by my office. And if I'm in a position to buy, I still might be interested." By the end of the day, however, I had put the offer out of my mind, foreseeing a messy, complicated process.

About a month later, the same man showed up at my office and said, "Fred, I've got that property available now if you're still interested."

"Let me see what I can do," I said. *Perhaps this was the answer to my prayer after all.*

The next day I got a call from the appraiser at Orange Savings and Loan saying he checked out the property, liked what he saw, and had a loan offer for me. Without even knowing, the offer was exactly the amount I needed.

This has to be God, I thought. The signs were all there, so I bought the building.

When escrow closed, I went down to introduce myself to the tenants as their new landlord. The first tenant I introduced myself to was the owner of the party supply store. When I told him who I was, he suddenly got really upset: "My mother-in-law had an option on this!" he yelled. "How could you buy this? She had an option!"

"Don't ask me," I said. "I didn't know anything about your mother-in-law. We just closed escrow today."

Well, you can imagine the man wasn't too satisfied with my answer. I did feel bad for him and his mother-in-law. At the same time, the whole situation reinforced in my mind that my purchase of this property was nothing short of a God thing, being in the nick of time.

Originally, I was going to tear everything down and put in a service station, but I realized the Spanish architecture was very similar to a development down the street called Town and Country across from Fashion Square. There was no need to tear everything down when I had a building that already suited the street; all it needed was some fixing up. I got rid of the beer bar and the pet store, whose leases were up anyway, and I removed all the modern modifications from the Spanish building and extended the Spanish motif across the rest of the property to give it more architectural beauty and uniformity. I was quite proud of the finished product.

I owned that property for forty years. All that while, the property appreciated in value. Because of the circumstances of how I got that building—it being a gift from God and all—it wasn't long into my ownership that I felt like I should give it back somehow. The community of Orange had always been good to me, and so in the back of my mind I figured that someday I would donate that property to St. Joseph's Hospital to show my appreciation for the town. Like I hinted at, when I first bought the property, I didn't have that much money in it and had no idea what kind of value it would come to in the future, so I tabled that dream for the time being.

Then in 1970 or thereabouts, I went into negotiations with St. Joseph's to set up a charitable remainder trust, meaning that when Ruth and I died, the property would pass on to the hospital. In the meantime, I'd still be earning income and what have you, and the hospital would pay me a return based on its value—a small amount of money compared to its total value.

The hospital's representative whom I was in contact with was a man named Gary Bourne. Prior to working at the hospital, Gary had worked for Biola University, a non-denominational Christian university with Presbyterian roots just north of Anaheim. Together Gary and I came up with the stipulations of the trust. The board turned it down, however, saying that the appraisal was $100,000 more than it should be.

When Gary came back with the amended proposal and told me what had happened, I was disappointed. I reminded him that I wasn't selling the property to them, I was giving it to them; the return they would pay me was only 5 percent of its total value. Now, if I had been in it solely for the money, I could have sold it full price. I told Gary, "Just tell them to forget it."

A couple of years later Gary left the hospital and went back to work for Biola. One day he came to me and said, "Fred, would you consider making that same deal with Biola?" By this time the market value had gone down a bit, which meant that the return wouldn't be as much. Knowing the property would be going to a Christian university, I said, "That would really fit far more into our Christian perspective and desires than for it to go to the hospital," although I did recognize that the hospital was a Catholic institution and a tremendous service to the community, which was why I had them in mind to begin with. But that was in the past. I made the deal with Biola, which I felt really good about.

Sometime after this, Biola got an offer from someone to buy the property, but they were asking for less than full price. They came to me about it, and I told them, "Before you go ahead with this offer, contact the hospital again to see if they're still interested." Sure enough they were—and they were willing to pay full price! In the end, Biola sold that property for $2 million!

As a result of my donating this property, I've been on a first-name basis with all of the Biola presidents ever since. In 2007 Barry Corey was selected as the university's tenth and current president. As a former Assemblies of God pastor, he was an interesting choice for president given that Biola was by and large cessationist—that is, believing that the gifts of the Holy Spirit had ended with the apostles. In truth, they were even quite cool to the charismatic way of life. Of course, the faculty was well aware of Barry's affiliation and personal beliefs, but we saw Barry's coming to Biola as a great sign for the university.

I had lunch with Barry early in his tenure, and after hearing that he was a Spirit-filled Christian, I pretty much shared my whole testimony with him. Through our friendship, God started opening up doors for me to speak at Biola about the baptism of the Holy Spirit and his gifts *that are for us today*. I've even prayed for students to receive the baptism of the Holy Spirit. Because I didn't work for Biola, I could say and do these things without it officially reflecting on the university, or on Barry. This opened the doors for understanding the work and ministry of the Holy Spirit.

I want to quickly tell you a testimony about another Biola professor who has come to some of our meetings. When Ruth and I made a generous donation to Talbot School of Theology to help build the new Talbot East building, they dedicated their new prayer chapel to us, naming it after us too. We told them not to put our names anywhere since we weren't looking for any recognition: "We just want to give it to God for his glory, not ours," but they did it nevertheless.

Anyway, I'm bringing this up because there was a Spirit-filled professor at Biola, who, when a couple of her students were going through some hardships, took her class to the prayer chapel to pray for these girls. This was the professor's first time to the brand-new chapel, and lo and behold, she recognized our names. (As an aside, I don't know what the girls' problems were exactly—something physical I believe—but they were delivered, praise God! Another divine encounter!)

For reasons we weren't aware of yet, our names were very important to this professor. She wrote us a letter following her time in the chapel. When we opened the letter, it read, "When I was a little girl, I lived across the street from you. Your wife had a club where she taught kids about Jesus." At this point Ruth and I knew that she was referring to my son, who shares my name. This would have been about forty years ago. The letter continued: "My brother and I went to your home and received Jesus into our lives. Not only that, but you invited my dad to go to Forest Home," a ministry our son operated for a time. "We weren't Christians, but my dad went. He committed his life to the Lord. I wanted you to know that my mom and dad, after all these years, are living for the Lord and are involved in the church and working for the Lord. I also wanted you to know that my life was changed when you invited me to your home to find Jesus. Now I'm all grown up and still a believer! I'm a professor at Biola, actually. I saw your name on the chapel, which prompted me to write you this letter."

We forwarded the letter to our son and then contacted this professor, explaining that Talbot had dedicated the prayer chapel to us, not to our son and his wife, which was a fun conversation. Even so, we told her we were tremendously blessed by her letter and invited her to come see us at the Ranch.

Ruth and I love encounters of this kind. Divine encounters. A little touch of heaven. This is why we do what we do, because when you share Jesus with people, you never know who God is going to touch or what fruits will come of it. You can trust God will move and that fruit will come to bear—even if that fruit comes years later.

The way I see it, all of this had its beginning with that simple prayer back in 1961, asking the Lord if he would lead me to a new work project. How could I have known it would snowball into all of this? It's baffling and wonderful to think about. It goes to show that you can't underestimate the power of a single prayer—even if it feels trivial. If your heart is in the right place, God can use any prayer for his kingdom. As with the mustard seed, which is the smallest of seeds, he has the power and the wisdom to make it grow into a mighty tree. God guided me to a real estate project that resulted in an opportunity for a university to have a more open view of the work and ministry of the Holy Spirit—all from my simple prayer. That's the power of God.

Nineteen

The Greens

Ruth:

IN THE EARLY eighties, our friends Betty and Bill Dumas introduced us to Keith Green's parents. This was about six months after Keith died in that tragic plane crash where two of his young children also died. It was so very sad. They were all such beautiful souls. Keith was such an anointed singer-songwriter.

The Dumases met the Greens while camping in Yosemite. They happened to park their motorhome right next to Char and Harvey's camper. Betty, a huge Keith Green fan, was playing one of his albums, when Char overheard her son's music next door and went over to introduce herself. I can only imagine how shocked Betty was when she realized Keith's parents were staying in the next camper over. The two couples became pretty good friends.

Keith Green

Sometime later Fred and I were invited by the Dumases to a dinner party celebrating their twenty-fifth anniversary. The Greens were also invited, and we were very excited to meet them, as we were also big fans of Keith and his music.

The day of the party, Fred and I left extra early just to be sure we wouldn't be late. The Greens, who apparently had the same idea, arrived just as we did. As we waited for Betty and Bill to arrive, we made small talk and got to know one another a little bit. Things were going really great for the time being. Then I made the mistake of bringing up Keith. I said, "Oh, we're so sorry to hear about your son. But isn't it wonderful that now he's with Jesus?"

Suddenly Char's face turned rigid, and in anger she burst out and yelled, "Don't say another word about him!"

Oh no! What did I do? I thought, absolutely mortified. I was only trying to express my sympathies and encourage them a little in their grief. However, I was unaware at that time that they weren't believers. Ethnically they were Jewish, but religiously they were Christian Scientists. In any case, Char obviously didn't share in the same hope for Keith that I knew to be true—that he was still alive, that he was with God. And grieving for her son, she wasn't in the mood to hear "wishful thinking." I also found out later that Betty had been witnessing to the Greens about the Lord, which probably explains why Char was so curt with me the second I brought up God: She was fed up with it all already.

Char didn't speak to us for the rest of the night. The tension was terrible! To make matters worse, we had to sit and wait for the Dumases to show up for another half hour! Thankfully Harvey didn't completely give us the cold shoulder and was gracious enough to talk to us while we waited, otherwise it would have been unbearable. But boy did it feel good when the Dumases showed up.

We didn't mention anything to Betty and Bill about what happened until after the dinner.

"Oh my goodness!" Betty said. "We need to get you guys together again. We need to fix this!"

"I don't know if that's such a good idea," I said. "I don't think Char wants anything to do with us."

"Don't worry. She'll come around," Betty said confidently.

So after we let things settle down a bit, we invited the Greens, along with the Dumases, to stay with us one weekend at our condo in Palm Springs as a sort of peace offering. The only condition was that everyone join us for church that Sunday. Char wasn't too enthusiastic about that part, but after a while Harvey convinced her to go.

The first couple of days at the condo were great. We didn't talk about the Lord or anything like that; we just wanted to be friendly and to keep things lighthearted. Friday and Saturday were all about having fun: We went riding around the golf course and later went to the fair. We made a lot of progress in getting to know Harvey and Char.

Then Sunday morning rolled around. We really wanted the Greens to check out a new church in Palm Springs that was led by a young couple and kind of an offshoot of the Vineyard. At the time, the Vineyard was like a wonderful spiritual explosion happening in Southern California, thanks to Lonnie and John Wimber.

So we got up early to get ready, had breakfast. When the Dumases came down dressed and ready, they asked, "Where's Char and Harvey?"

"It looks like they're not even up," I said. "I haven't heard a sound from their room."

"Well, it's almost time to go. What're we going to do?" asked Betty.

"Maybe we should wake them up," Fred suggested.

Just then Harvey came walking down the stairs, still in his pajamas.

I said, "Oh, Harvey, aren't you and Char coming to church with us? We're about to leave."

Harvey seemed caught off guard by the question. "But we're not dressed for church," he said.

"Harvey, you don't have to dress up to go to this church," I said reassuringly. "It's mostly young people; they come just like they are. Now go get Char. We'll wait for you."

So Harvey went back upstairs and made quick work in persuading Char to get ready and head out to church with us.

We got to the church a little late; there were hardly any open seats left. As we looked for a place to sit, the worship band was playing a song that sounded very familiar to me. It was a Keith

Green song! I couldn't believe it. I glanced at Char to see if it had sunk in yet: By the look of her it had.

Still looking for a place to sit, we saw that the only available seats left were in the very front row. Thinking the Greens wouldn't want to sit so far up, I told the usher trying to help us, "It's okay, we'll just stand back here for now." But then Char said, "Oh no. Let's go up to the front," and off she went, leading the way, no questions asked. *She's a woman of action*, I thought. *I like that.* It was so comical, so like Char.

Two more of Keith's songs were played during worship. I could tell it was a special moment for Harvey and Char, feeling the love for their son from complete strangers in that place. Meanwhile, my level of expectation was going up and up because it was clear as day to me that God brought the Greens to this church that morning for a very specific purpose: a divine encounter. When the service ended, the Greens made a beeline for the pastor. They found out from him that he and his wife had been good friends with Keith and his wife, Melody. It was the happiest I had seen Char and Harvey. I think for them it was like being close to their son again, like finding a secret diary of his. The whole time I was thinking, *Oh, God, please let them get saved today!* And I was so sure they *would* be saved. How could they not after a morning like that? How could they not see that God was calling them? The signs were all over the place.

I was still in the dark as to whether or not they accepted Christ when we left. I didn't want to ask, because I was worried I might upset Char again, so I asked the pastor a few days later what happened. He told me that unfortunately they hadn't accepted Christ that morning.

Oh well, I thought. *At least a seed was planted that day.*

In any case, it had been a fantastic weekend for all of us. I had nothing to be sad about.

The next time we hung out with the Greens was when we took up their invitation to go motorhome camping with them and the

Dumases in Malibu. We brought Linda with us as well as her ten-year-old daughter, and the Dumases brought their granddaughter with them, who was around the same age as our granddaughter. It was a nice little gathering of friends and family in beautiful Malibu. Can't get any better than that, right?

This was our first time camping in Malibu, so when we showed up to the campsite, we weren't sure where to park our motorhome. The Dumases, who had arrived a little bit before us, told us to park right next to them. We had everything set up and ready for the next few days of camping, when the Greens showed up with some of their friends in tow; then Char rolled down her passenger window and said, "You guys are in our spot."

Oh no! I hope they don't think we're trying to steal their spot, I thought. *And I hope this doesn't set us back with the Greens any.*

But Fred handled it really well. "No problem. We'll move right away," he said.

We moved to an open spot across the street. It was a little bit of an inconvenience since we were separated from the group now, but we weren't bothered by it. Our main focus was drawing the Greens to Christ.

That first night we made a big bonfire and all gathered around it doing bonfire things. The kids immediately gravitated toward Harvey, who was such a softy and a big kid himself. In fact, every chance the girls could get to play with Harvey during the trip, they took it. He'd chase them around or help them cook their marshmallows over the bonfire. In the mornings the girls would run over to Char and Harvey's camper, knock on their camper door, and yell, "Harvey! Come out and play!" It was so cute. And Harvey was such a good sport about it. He'd take them hiking and play all sorts of games with them throughout the day.

As for the rest of us, Linda and I continued our usual morning devotionals that we had started at some point after she was diagnosed with MS and was forced to move in with us. She was in her thirties, and by this point she was suffering severely from her disease, confined to a wheelchair. She could hardly do anything for herself, having lost just about all control of her body. But like Fred said, it didn't get her down one bit; she was an angel.

Char fell absolutely in love with Linda, who ended up joining us most mornings for our devotionals. Char loved to brush Linda's hair or fix her nails. More importantly, she was amazed by how happy and full of life Linda was despite her condition and was charmed by how much Linda looked forward to her daily devotionals.

"And you do this every morning?" Char asked.

"Mhm. Every morning," Linda said. "I love it."

It was a win-win situation for me: Linda was making a friend, and Char was getting to hear Scripture and to see for herself what a relationship with Christ was all about (which, by the way, is sometimes no more complicated than being more intentional about your mornings). I felt like this was exactly the kind of Christian witness Char needed—the subtle, more natural approach.

But then on the last night of the trip, things went wrong. It all started when Betty told me she had thought of a really good idea.

"What is it?" I asked.

"Well, first: Can you make a dessert for tonight? I want to throw a dessert party in our motorhome to finish out the trip."

"Sure—but what's the big idea?"

"So, while we're all eating dessert," she explained, "I'm going to put on this really good tape for Harvey and Char to listen to: It's going to teach them that they need to have a relationship with the Lord."

Uh oh, I instantly thought. *I'm not sure Char's going to like this.* But I kept my mouth shut. *Well, Char has had some positive exposure to Christianity since the first time we met; maybe she's ready for a more direct approach again.* I decided to just go with it and see what happened.

That night, while we were all having dessert and enjoying one another's company, Betty did just as she said she would. She asked everyone to sit down. "I want to play something for everyone," she said. My heart started beating fast. *This will either go really good or really bad,* I thought. *Please, God, help it to go good!*

Betty put on the tape. When it became clear what kind of tape it was and that it wasn't exactly intended for everyone, Char shot up and yelled, "That's it! We're out of here!"

"But, Char, what's wrong?" Betty asked, immediately turning off the tape.

Char didn't even answer her question. She just said, "I will never speak to you again!" and then stormed out of the motorhome. Of course Harvey, caught in the unfortunate middle, followed after her.

No one said anything for a while. The party was officially over; suddenly the dessert didn't taste so good anymore. We all knew we had crossed a certain line that shouldn't have been crossed. We had quite literally lured our friends with desserts into trying to convert them! Of course, we didn't think of it that way at the time. We just wanted them to know the Lord. But we learned the hard way that the means don't always justify the ends. Now we weren't sure the Greens would ever talk to us again.

After a little time passed, Fred went out to find Harvey and Char. They were sitting by the fire, looking pretty sour. Fred apologized and then explained that Betty hadn't meant any harm by what she did: "Betty loves you guys and wants the best for you. No one's trying to force you to become Christians. And we're not going to quit being friends if you don't believe what we believe. It doesn't work that way; God doesn't work that way. But at the same time, for us, for born-again Christians, nothing is more important than seeing our loved ones and our friends get saved. More than just this earthly life is at stake, and so it would be a disgrace if we didn't try to tell as many people as we could about the love of Christ. We're not trying to coerce you into anything; we're just trying to love you the best way we know how."

Fred was able to cool down Char for the most part, and things went back to normal—except that Char refused to forgive Betty. In fact, for a good while she stuck to her word that she never wanted to speak to Betty again.

Now, with everything that had happened, you'd think Betty would have let up with the whole preaching thing and learned her lesson by now. But she hadn't. She kept "knocking at the door," you could say. That was the kind of person Betty was. Keith had written a song called "I Only Want To See You There." It was about Keith's hope and prayer that his parents would be in heaven when he got there. Of course, I'm sure Keith thought his parents would be the ones waiting for him in heaven, not the other way around. Regardless of how it sadly turned out, his prayer remained the same.

I think Betty's love for Keith and the fact that God had brought her and the Greens together compelled Betty to do everything she could to see Keith's prayer fulfilled. I believe she believed part of her purpose was to bring the Greens to Christ, and no amount of rejection was going to stop her.

Eventually Char softened up, or Betty wore her down, and they were friends again. For a while things were back to normal. We were all hanging out again. But then Harvey got really sick and was put in the hospital. Betty—bless her soul—visited him regularly.

One day when Betty visited Harvey in the hospital, Char happened to be gone, running some errands or something of the sort. This was the opportunity Betty was looking for, apparently, because she asked Harvey if he would like to accept Jesus into his heart.

"I would," he said from his hospital bed.

"Repeat after me," Betty said with great joy.

When Char came back a little later, Harvey exclaimed, "Oh, Char! It's so wonderful! It's Jesus! He's real! And it's so wonderful!" Char didn't take the news very well. I don't think she appreciated

Betty going behind her back like that, at least that's how she saw it. Once again Char was no longer on speaking terms with Betty.

Sadly, Harvey died soon after. Death is always a tragedy, but Christ defeated death, and in him that victory becomes ours. In other words, Harvey defeated death that day in the hospital because the Author of Life, the One who had already died and resurrected, entered into Harvey's heart and gave Harvey the gift of eternal life, which is Christ himself. "Most assuredly, I say to you, if anyone keeps my word he shall never see death," Jesus said in the Gospel of John. And also, "Now this is eternal life, that they may know you, the only true God, and Jesus Christ whom you have sent."[10]

There's probably nothing more infuriating to the devil than when someone repents on his or her deathbed, and at the same time, nothing that makes those in heaven happier. I'm sure Keith was beyond overjoyed to see his dad walk through those pearly gates and into his embrace. Now they could wait for Char together.

Not long after Harvey passed, Char got sick. Since Betty wasn't seeing much of Char at that time, she called me up one day and asked if Linda and I would do her a favor and go visit Char in the hospital. "Of course," I said. "I'm sure seeing Linda would make her so happy."

During our visit I felt the Lord prompting me to share Christ with her one more time.

"Wouldn't you like to accept Jesus and know that you have hope in heaven?" I asked. "And you'd get to be with Harvey and your son."

"Yes, I would," she said softly.

Praise the Lord! Finally! I thought with total glee. *Another divine encounter!*

And so we prayed together in that hospital room, like Betty had with Harvey, and Char received Jesus into her heart. It was so beautiful.

Then I said, "Char, you know, you need to have the power of the Holy Spirit to really live this new life now. Would you like to be baptized with the Holy Spirit?"

"Yes, yes, yes! I would!" she exclaimed.

I added, "When I pray for you, if you feel the need to let anything out, just let it flow."

"Okay," she said.

Before I had even finished praying, she started speaking in tongues—and so naturally and beautifully too. There was no hesitation in her at all. I was so happy! I couldn't wait to tell Betty.

Then it hit me: Keith's prayer had been answered! Or at least it would be. Did he know already? It says in the Bible that angels rejoice in heaven over the salvation of sinners: Do people rejoice with them? It's hard for me to imagine angels keeping such good news to themselves. I wish I could have seen Keith's and Harvey's faces when the angels gave them the good news that Char was saved. What a beautiful scene that probably was. But how much more beautiful the moment they were all reunited together in heaven when Char passed away two months later. I'm sure the first ones to welcome her were Keith and Harvey. Sometimes I think about them having a blast up there. I can't wait to see Char and Harvey again and Keith for the first time (maybe he'll play me a song or two) when it's my turn to pass from this life to the next—into eternity!

Twenty

Finishing the Race

Fred:

RUTH AND I have witnessed a number of incredible moves of God. We've also been privileged to be a part of some. This heartfelt account has detailed some of the highlights of our long journey. Through it all Jesus has literally captured our lives and our hearts. It is now the year 2020, and we both recently turned ninety-eight years old. How time flies! Have you noticed?

We have been asked what we feel is the main message of our lives and what we would like to impart to anyone reading our story. In this closing chapter we will both respond to that question. Ruth and I are one in Christ and one in marriage but still have many unique perspectives and special experiences. God is so creative and loving and meets all our needs, hopes, and dreams individually as well as within a well-seasoned marriage of seventy-nine years.

Both of us love to see God touch people who are running in the opposite direction. He touches them with his reality and love in so many ways. Our Father God has supernaturally demonstrated this love by sending his only begotten Son, Jesus the Christ, into our world.

> But as many as *received him*, to them gave he power to become the sons of God, even to them that believe on his name: Which were born, not of blood, nor of the will of the flesh, nor of the will of man, but of God.[11]

This scripture reveals that we become "born again" by receiving and believing in Jesus!

As much as Ruth and I positively love to see people initially encounter God and become sincere born-again believers and disciples of Christ, we have also been given a very special burden with a focus on the role of the Holy Spirit in all of our lives. In Acts 2 we read of a divine encounter that changed the kingdom of God forever, which eventually became known as the day of Pentecost. Everyone needs to consume the truths in this chapter as well as the rest of the Scriptures. Receiving the power and anointing from the Holy Spirit to live a fruitful, overcoming life is so vitally important. For us, it is the main message that we would like people to take away from our lives.

For two thousand years now people around the world have celebrated Jesus's resurrection, his conquering of death itself, on Easter Sunday. But for forty days before his ascension back to heaven, Jesus shared many revelations and instructions to his disciples and also to multiple crowds of people. Probably the most penetrating instruction for Ruth and me has been the very last words Jesus spoke on earth:

> And ye are witnesses of these things. And, behold, I send the promise of my Father upon you: but tarry ye in the city of Jerusalem, until ye be endued with power from on high. And he led them out as far as to Bethany, and he lifted up his hands, and blessed them. And it came to pass, while he blessed them, he was parted from them, and carried up into heaven. And they worshipped him, and returned to Jerusalem with great joy.[12]

Ruth:

As Fred mentioned we have the detailed story of the very first major outpouring of the Holy Spirit in the Book of Acts on the day of Pentecost. We love to proclaim, especially to young believers, how important and wonderful it is to be "endued with power from on high!" Previous to Pentecost, Jesus had commanded his disciples:

"Do not leave Jerusalem, but wait for the gift my Father promised, which you have heard me speak about. For John baptized with water, but in a few days you will be baptized with the Holy Spirit."[13]

Fred and I experienced this wonderful baptism of the Holy Spirit ourselves many long decades ago. To the best of our ability we have tried in this book to share with you the many blessings that have followed. It revolutionized our walk with God—and actually has become our passion. It gives us, and all who want to serve God, the anointing and power to be faithful witnesses. You know, there are nine special gifts of the Holy Spirit listed in the Bible, which include the word of wisdom, the word of knowledge, faith, gifts of healing, miracles, prophecy, distinguishing of spirits, tongues, and the interpretation of tongues.[14] Each one of these gifts is very supernatural from God and incredibly powerful. Unfortunately, many people and even certain denominations have somewhat been scared away by one of the most accessible and important gifts, which is our prayer language, the gift of tongues. But what a difference the gifts have been to our lives. In fact, all nine have been demonstrated to be part of this controversial "baptism of fire," which is available to every believer. On the day of Pentecost itself, while Peter was preaching, the Holy Spirit fell on a huge crowd with cloven tongues of fire appearing over each person as they began speaking in other languages. It sent a shock wave through Jerusalem and around the world to this very day!

We want anyone who reads our story to say, "Oh, I want this! I want this enduement of power for myself!" That's truly what we would love to see happen! We feel a special call of God to inspire young people to have a closer walk. While we were working with Lonnie in Riverside, he would preach at All Saints, leading hundreds of kids to Jesus, and then after the service many of us, mostly teenagers and young adults, would caravan to our house. Lonnie, along with Fred and I and sometimes other leaders, would introduce everyone to the baptism of the Holy Spirit. We had so many wild, Spirit-filled, amazing meetings in our home, and even now so many years later, Lonnie's close friend, John Ruttkay, continues with life-changing meetings in our home. Well into our nineties, we are still available and going strong.

The apostle Peter is actually our greatest example of the need for the baptism of the Holy Spirit. Before he received this experience, he denied Jesus three times. Peter thought he was strong and even told Jesus the night before his crucifixion, "I would never leave you, and I would even die for you!" But when confronted later, he cursed and swore, "I don't even know the man!" We want to protect our young people who confess salvation but don't have the baptism of the Holy Spirit. When the test comes, they could easily be as weak as Peter and deny him. Instead, we want them to be like Peter on the day of Pentecost. When the Holy Spirit fell on him and the crowd, Peter boldly preached with a powerful anointing and led three thousand people to Christ! We want our young ones to be emboldened with that kind of power and anointing from on high. Right now I can hear Jesus say, "This baptism of the Holy Spirit is for you to go and be my witnesses."

Fred:

There have been two great outpourings, or "waves," of the Holy Spirit in America in the twentieth century. The first wave began with the Pentecostal movements of Azusa Street and then of Aimee Semple McPherson (both in LA) soon after. As mentioned early in this book, I have a direct connection to this revival, primarily in my mother, who was baptized in the Holy Spirit at McPherson's church back in the late 1920s. The second wave was the charismatic movement that began with Oral Roberts and the televangelists and then culminated with the Jesus People movement of the sixties and seventies. I played a minor role in both of these movements: First, having worked for Oral for a number of years at ORU; second, in the relationships I had over the years with a number of key people in the Jesus People movement, including Lonnie Frisbee, Kenn Gulliksen, Greg Laurie, and John Wimber.

It's definitely not my intention to boast, but rather to point out that, for whatever reason, God orchestrated all of this—for his glory. I also can't help wondering if God will have Ruth and I play some role in the next great movement. We aren't getting any younger, that's for sure! Our time is nearly up. And yet our hearts yearn to see the Holy Spirit move in a big way again before we go. We want to see this much-anticipated third wave! The church is going on fifty years now since the last great revival, at least as far as America is concerned. In any case, the whole world needs another great move of God, another divine encounter. Times seem darker than ever. Our world is absolutely going mad with rage, violence, lawlessness, and confusion. Is this the prophesied end of an age?

The Scriptures say that in the "end days" there will be a tremendous ingathering of souls right before the coming of the Lord.[15] The world has seen many manifestations of that promise, beginning with Pentecost, but time has kept marching on. The Lord is still biding his time, "not wanting anyone to perish, but everyone to come to repentance."[16] Countless believers have come and gone. Many believed they would personally see the return of Jesus before they died. The apostles themselves thought they would witness that great day—and it's been two thousand years since. Were they wrong? No, because as Peter reminds us, "with the Lord one day is like a thousand years, and a thousand years like one day."[17] So when it comes to the concept of time, "near" and "far" have deeper eschatological meanings and realities than merely having to do with chronological time.

Of course, we old folks need the younger generations to take the torch and run with it; we can't rely on the fumes of past revivals to get us where we need to go. The next huge move of the Spirit has to come out of a generation's own encounter with God. Trying to rebottle the past for the present takes our focus off of what God, who is always at work in our midst, is already doing. That isn't to say we shouldn't let the past inspire or inform us; but if we expect the next revival to happen the way it did forty or fifty years ago, we're severely limiting the power and freedom of God to work through us. There's no formula to guaranteeing a revival. They seem to happen when we least expect them to.

As you can see, it's unwise to presume the mind of God. We can't predict when God will "show up" or even how. But we can ready ourselves for that day. We can be like Simeon, "who was righteous and devout. . . . waiting for the consolation of Israel," and who, when he saw the newly born Jesus in the temple, instantly recognized him as the Messiah.[18] We can also be like the prophetess Anna, who, after being widowed early in her life, "never left the temple but worshiped night and day, fasting and praying" until she was eighty-four years old.[19] Due to her faithfulness and love for God, who had been seemingly absent from his people for centuries, she also recognized Jesus as the Christ.

Like these admirable individuals, our expectations should always be exceedingly high when it comes to God's promise to perform mighty works in our world, but we can't let our expectations blind us. We must expect the unexpected. Israel greatly expected the Messiah, but very few recognized him when he came. They were stuck in the past, so to speak. Likewise, many of us think we know what the future will look like. We read passages about the end times and think we have a clear idea how it's going to unfold in real time. More than likely, those passages will be fulfilled in ways we never would have guessed. Their fulfillment will far exceed our expectations; they'll make our expectations look laughable and superficial.

I think this is the kind of mindset we should have going into the next revival, whenever it happens. Obviously, something isn't new if it's been done before. This isn't to say that we should all abandon our stuck-in-their-ways churches for cutting-edge ones. God isn't looking for innovation, he's looking for faithfulness. God's the Innovator, the One who creates out of nothing. All of our methodologies and strategies for church growth or evangelism or revival are fools' errands if they don't have at their center humility and love for the untamable God we serve.

On the other hand, then, we're deceiving ourselves if we think God is interested in working only with what's new and popular or with the smartest or most talented. God created man out of dust and woman from a rib—things which by themselves are nothing. God created a people unto himself from nothing in order to bless the nations. He brought Egypt, the world's superpower of the time, to its knees with a bunch of slaves. Israel's greatest king, David, was a nobody, a young shepherd. God chose a poor young virgin from a nowhere village to bear the King of Kings and Lord of Lords. Even the Son of God came as a "nobody," the son of a carpenter, poor and unremarkable. Jesus chose for himself a motley group of unimpressive and socially despised individuals for his disciples. And after Jesus ascended and commissioned his disciples, the number of so-called nobodies coming into the faith—the poor, women, the formerly diseased and disfigured, slaves, Gentiles, the barren, the powerless—grew like wildfire, until eventually these nobodies, whom everyone thought were strange, or ridiculous, or a blight on society, spread across the known world and beyond.

God's not afraid to use the foolish things of the world to confound the wise.[20] As James writes, "Has not God chosen the poor in this world to be rich in faith and heirs of the kingdom that He promised to those loving him?"[21] Our power, our riches, our intelligence, our earthly wisdom—these are nothing if we think we can outwit God or if we're deluded enough to think we can make him work for *us*. Our job, thankfully, is very simple: to plant and to water. The Father has given us the Seed: his Son; and he's given us the Water: Christ's own words and deeds of eternal life, upborne by the Spirit, who lives in us. And for a clincher, it's God who gives the growth. Can anyone, therefore, boast in and of themselves? If we are faithful to do our small part—which is an honor, really, to be coworkers of God—then God will be faithful to do his.

The revival will come, a huge ingathering of souls. It's on its way. The angels are on the move. Whether or not I see it with my own eyes and hear it with my own ears matters very little in the grand scheme of it all. I know by God's grace I've had a small part in getting the world to the shores of a new heaven and a new earth, and I know that as long as Ruth and I are alive, we'll always have a part to play in ushering in the kingdom. Paul says, "I consider my life worth nothing to me; my only aim is to finish the race and complete the task the Lord Jesus has given me—the task of testifying to the good news of God's grace."[22] Later on, while imprisoned, not long before his martyrdom, Paul writes to Timothy:

> I have fought the good fight, I have finished the race, I have kept the faith. Now there is in store for me the crown of righteousness, which the Lord, the righteous Judge, will award to me on that day—and not only me, but also to all who have longed for his appearing.[23]

Like Paul, Ruth and I long for the glorious appearing of our Lord and Savior. We want to be able to say, as he did, that we have finished the race and have kept the faith until the very end, recognizing that it was not of our own doing, but by God's bountiful grace. This is why we do what we do. This is why we still have our meetings with young people in our home, which continue to grow and bear fruit. This is why we need to tell people about Jesus and the Holy Spirit. Our personal race isn't over until all agency to promote the gospel is taken from us; and if and when that happens, God take us quickly!

The next great move of the Spirit can't happen without God, but it certainly won't happen without his people either. God is interested in saving us, not just cleaning us up; he's interested in empowering us for *his* world, which is here *now* and coming very *soon.*

I want to leave you with a picture of Jesus and a crowd of his disciples on his last day on earth as he ascended:

> They were looking intently up into the sky as he was going, when suddenly two men dressed in white stood beside them. "Men of Galilee," they said, "why do you stand here looking into the sky? This same Jesus, who has been taken from you into heaven, will come back in the same way you have seen him go into heaven."[24]

Ruth and I love each and every one of you with the precious love of the risen Christ Jesus of Nazareth. As Ruth often says, "We look forward to seeing you here, there, or in the air when Jesus comes. Keep looking up!" Shalom my friends. May you have many divine encounters.

Notes

[1] Matthew 5:48 NKJV

[2] Acts 2:39 KJV

[3] Matthew 26:41 NIV

[4] Matthew 7:9–11 NKJV

[5] Matthew 6:20 NIV

[6] John 14:6; 10:7–11

[7] 2 Cor. 6:2 NIV

[8] Genesis 50:20 NIV

[9] Children of the Day, "For Those Tears I Died," track B5 on *Come to the Waters*, Maranatha! Music, 1971, vinyl LP.

[10] John 17:3 NIV

[11] John 1:12–13 KJV

[12] Luke 24:48–52 KJV

[13] Acts 1:4–5 NIV

[14] 1 Corinthians 12:7–10

[15] Joel 2:28–32

[16] 2 Peter 3:9 NIV

[17] 2 Peter 3:8 NASB

[18] Luke 2:25 NIV

[19] Luke 2:37 NIV

[20] 1 Cor. 1:27

[21] James 2:5 BLB

[22] Acts 20:24 NIV

[23] 2 Tim. 4:7–8 NIV

[24] Acts 1:10 NIV

About the Authors

FRED AND RUTH WAUGH are spiritual parents to generations and have devoted their lives to seeing people experience the reality of the Holy Spirit today. They love spending time with their grandchildren and great-grandchildren and hosting prayer meetings at their ranch in Riverside, CA.

JOHN SACHS is a native of Southern California. In 2016, he graduated from California Baptist University with a Master of Arts degree in English. He has been working for Freedom Crusade as a writer ever since, and currently lives in Santa Maria, CA, with his beloved wife and two children.

Made in the USA
Coppell, TX
05 June 2021